ACCOLADES FOR AGILI

"Agile Strategy Execution is an invaluable resource highlighting the role of process in strategy delivery. The guidance, tools and approaches are presented in a simple and intuitive way, making them readily usable to bring strategy to life and ensure critical cultural engagement, alignment, accountability and responsiveness that ultimately delivers the results." – ***Craig Shields, Senior Director, Global Operations Strategy, Abbott Medical Optics***

"Being a small firm in a fiercely competitive market, agile strategy execution is critical to our success. Using the principles outlined in this book as a guide, in less than 12 months, we have been able to successfully assess and improve our approach in some really innovative ways." – ***Jared Hamilton, CEO - Driving Sales***

"Modern organizations need to worry about different dimensions of performance to be successful—strategy formulation, strategic alignment and strategy execution, to name a few. Agile Strategy Execution makes a nice contribution to the dialogue around developing modern management systems that help organizations improve their performance. Read this book and you'll learn new things that you can apply in your organization to good effect." – ***Howard Rohm, President and CEO of the Balanced Scorecard***

"Clemson and Leeds have really hit on something big here. I like their approach because it is grounded in deep theory covering leadership, culture, quality, and project management execution best practices. They provide real-world applications of the theory and the work is peppered throughout with specific examples that help key concepts 'come alive'. Their practical and straightforward approach hones in on the key challenges in strategy execution with new innovations in the areas of 'agile thinking' and Connected Governance.™ I'd recommend this book for anyone engaged in setting strategic direction and managing execution of strategies." – ***Jim Stockmal, President - Association for Strategic Planning***

"I have been an early adopter of this approach to agile strategy execution including using Agile Strategy Manger for quite some time. I have found its usefulness extends beyond managing your company's strategy. This centralization and 24/7 accessibility of vital information accelerate the decision-making process. It allows for increased efficiency and profitability by granting every user the opportunity to evaluate his or her goals, execute key initiatives, and ultimately optimize company performance globally. I view ASE as communication framework that has assisted me in managing my entire business " – ***Joel Welde, President, Medical Indicators Inc.***

"I have found many of the ASE framework, principles and techniques to be very useful in developing, refreshing and coordinating the global strategies for our 25 divisions and 230 geographic communities. It's a really innovative contribution to the field."
– Ha Dao, ASQ Member-Board of Directors, Co-Chair ASQ Strategic Planning Committee, & Technical Quality Manager, Emerson

"When it comes to execution most organizations are sloppy. The costs to our economy, to employee engagement, and to the delivery of value to customers and our society are staggering. Imagine leading a learning organization that thinks AND acts strategically--at every level, and with the capacity to improve execution EVERY year. Imagine a set of best practices to provide a path to new levels of excellence in your organization. Then read this book!"
– James L. Koch, Don C. Dodson Distinguished Service Professor of Management, Former Dean of the Leavey School of Business and Founder of the Miller Center for Social Entrepreneurship at Santa Clara University

"This book has been a valuable asset for me as an internal strategy practitioner interested in improving strategy execution throughout our organization." – ***Shannon Lechtenberg, Corporate Strategy and Business Planner - Great River Energy***

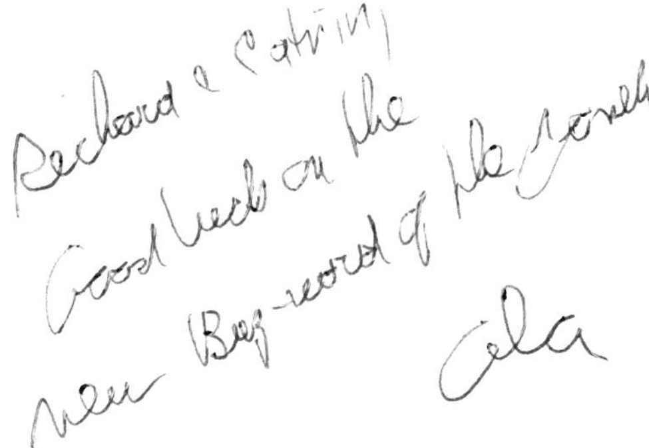

AGILE STRATEGY EXECUTION

REVOLUTIONIZING THE HOW!

By Gaye I. Clemson

and Alan J. Leeds

First Edition

Published in the United States and Canada through CreateSpace and Kindle Direct Publishing.

ISBN-13: 978-1537477633

ISBN-10: 1537477633

Table of Contents

FOREWORD & ACKNOWLEDGEMENTS

FOREWORD

Innovation often comes by what, in hindsight, seems pretty simple. In discussing innovation at Oxford University's Saïd Business School, Prof. Mark Ventresca quoted William Gibson[1], in saying that *"The future is already here — it's just not very evenly distributed."* Ventresca was describing architectural innovation – assembling that which already exists in new ways. The Agile Strategy Execution Framework™ is just that. Many of the ideas, methods, and concepts are well proven. Readers should take comfort in that they aren't being asked to toss out everything they know, but simply look at what they know in a new way. The Agile Strategy Execution Framework™ shifts us from a linear way of thinking to a virtuous cycle. Clemson & Leeds take a more realistic, real-world view of many of the strategy related processes, incorporating the reality of emergent strategy and the real world pressures of a complex, disruptive, changing world. Clemson & Leeds also bring new insights, such as Connected Governance™.

Others have tried to tackle these real-world pressures by advocating for simple linear speed. Simplifying the complex down to *execute faster* to complete the program or project, with its expected value greatly diminished. Clemson & Leeds advocate for agility, which accelerates execution, but agility isn't just about speed – it is about flexibility, adjusting midstream, and getting to the results we expect from our strategy, not simply calling a program or project *complete*. Agile Strategy Execution will help you to gain the expected value from your strategy, and that will be a game changer for you, your firm, and your customers. – ***Chris Hafner, Board of Trustees Chair & Fellow at the Strategic Planning Society, Board Member, Association for Strategic Planning, Lead Examiner/Fellow, Institute of Directors, President at Newton Consulting.***

---

1 The Science in Science Fiction on Talk of the Nation, NPR (30 November 1999, Timecode 11:55

ACKNOWLEDGEMENTS

When we started on this journey, nearly a decade ago, little did we know where the adventure would take us. In 2007, Gaye was with Cisco Systems, trying to find an automated way to link project and program activities to a newly minted, long-range strategic plan for the Technical Services Division. Alan, being in both consulting and the software business, was an expert in strategic planning, project, program and portfolio management and strategy performance management digitization. But it wasn't until about eight months ago, when *magic* happened. Senior leaders, clients and stakeholders were lamenting, more assertively than normal, about the lack of a way to apply agile software development principles to the way they ran their businesses. The thinking was that maybe agile concepts could drive, more effectively, strategy execution. We both had been involved in strategic planning and strategy execution for many years, and knew that there were many tools and techniques out there to help in the process. There was not, however, an inclusive framework that laid out precisely how to make strategy execution management efforts more agile. This book is an attempt to do just that.

Like Alice, in Alice in Wonderland, we've had some ideas grow very large and others that we thought should be large, grow very small. There have been times when we've wanted to throttle each other, and others when the joy and excitement of innovation and synergistic deep thinking have been mutually contagious. Now that our Agile Strategy Execution Framework™ has taken final form, it has been exciting to see that our ideas are generating even more contagious excitement amongst our fellow strategy execution practitioners and senior management leaders. It has been gratifying to see demonstrable client and colleague success.

As a result, we wanted to take a few minutes to acknowledge all of the support that we have received along the way from so many colleagues. Firstly, we'd like to thank organizations such as the ASP (Association for Strategic Planning), the ASQ (American Society of Quality), the Agile Alliance, the PMI (Project Management Institute) and the Stanford Center for Professional Development-IPS Learning, who encouraged us to come and present our ideas at their national and local conferences and chapters. Secondly, we'd like to thank strategy execution leaders who assisted in the refinement/design and execution of these concepts in their organizations. These include Shannon Lechtenberg from Great River Energy, Irfaan Kalyani from Abbott Medical Optics, Raj Saxena from Amazon, Ken Ketch from GroupMind Express, Don Siler and Bret Dupuis from Cisco Systems, Jim Stockmal, David Wells, David Thompson and the late Raffi Kamal (leading strategy consultants in their respective fields), and Laurie Bacopolous from Cobblestone. Thirdly, are Jeri and Eric Denniston from the Denner Group, Vidhyasagar Chandramohan and Lois Leeds who helped shape the final manuscript. Last, but not least, are those senior leaders who have inspired and constantly made us prove that these concepts would work in their environments. These include Craig Shields from Abbott Medical Optics, Jared Hamilton from Driving Sales, Ha Dao from ASQ, and of course our biggest fan and critic, Joel Welde, now President of Medical Indicators Inc.

We expect that as this framework is used, additional learnings will take place, so we encourage all to join our LinkedIn Group (Agile Strategy Execution) (https://www.linkedin.com/groups/17070549) to share those experiences. We believe strongly that only by deep collaboration can we progress and improve our skills at *pulling rabbits out of hats*, which at the moment, only Alan, as our resident professional magician, can do. Our experience has been that only by deep collaboration can we progress and move the journey together onwards in a positive way. Please feel free to reach out directly via info@agilestrategymanager.com or info@globalinkage.net.

PROLOGUE

A Large High Tech Company has just appointed a new Vice President of Operations who has just finished her first 30-day *listening* tour. Like many before, her conclusions sound something like this. *"What a great business we have here with incredible opportunity and profit potential! The strategy seems pretty solid and the team pretty smart, so it looks to me that with a little more focus and the setting of some priorities, we could really change the growth trajectory for this business!"*

There are, though, a few small warning signs that she has missed. The expected business outcomes, for example, have little substance and are really more aspirational in nature. The leadership team makes all kinds of decisions, but nobody knows about them. Frequently, team meetings degenerate into heated discussions as to whose *facts* are right. There is a lot of head nodding in the meeting, but many things seem to fall through the cracks and often action items don't seem to be getting done. Too often, last-minute

Hail Mary passes that generate success are being rewarded, not vilified, and little time is spent understanding what could be done differently so as to not have those late night conference calls. Problem solving looks more like 5-year olds playing soccer with everyone going after the ball all at the same time.

A Regional U.S. Power Supplier generates annually over 3700 megawatts in capacity that is delivered to over 1.7 million consumers. The head of Strategy and Planning can see that even with nearly $2 billion in revenue, there are some thunderstorms on the horizon. Electricity generation is still a priority, but the use of coal-based resources rather than natural gas or renewables is becoming a challenge. Moreover, his firm needs to figure out how to thrive in a world of declining costs. In addition, there are a growing number of consumers who want to operate *off the grid* with electric cars and home based solar energy storage mechanisms and a need to better support the existing infrastructure from physical and cyber threats. In his planning world, all reporting is based on Word and Excel and is out of date as of the date it is published. With limited vertical alignment, finding assigned work goals and actions is cumbersome and there is little line of sight from work goals to strategy. There are even looser links between strategy, work planning and the resources needed to achieve set goals in a timely manner.

A small, innovative and fast-growing Automotive Business Services Firm has built a suite of products to deliver innovative analytics and insight to help car dealerships optimize their businesses, solve their most pressing problems and optimize the performance of their people. This they do through competency assessments, structured learning and optimization, benchmarking, as well as a global online collaboration and support network to help individual dealership professionals grow in their careers. They exist in a fast moving market, with few staff members, and need to execute their software development and marketing projects quickly and with as much agility as possible with constant course corrections. With no legacy systems or processes, the President has a blank slate with which to use the latest and greatest best practices for strategy execution. He's hoping to not just leapfrog the competition, but also lead the industry in the use of real-time digital experience based management techniques, whilst building a culture that will attract awesome talent.

All three of these scenarios have a number of things in common. One is awareness of how difficult it is to drive effective strategy execution. Time and again, all three of these executives see trends happening that they want to exploit but are unable to leverage those opportunities. Another is that they hold annual strategic planning off-sites and quarterly planning meetings that yield great enthusiasm that isn't sustainable or doesn't deliver the results expected. More importantly, they notice how often company needs become subordinate to department self-interest or only address short-term issues. Everyone is working hard and fast, but concrete, measurable performance-driven results are elusive. Goals are missed, and no one can quite understand or explain why.

Unfortunately, industry research well reflects the reality of these concerns and suggests that they have been around for a long time, over 20 years in fact. It was in 1994 that Alan was first involved with *agile concepts* through the Agility Forum, which was a joint effort funded by DARPR and Lehigh University. The group's mission was to develop benchmarks that would help companies *"thrive in an environment of continuous and often unanticipated change."* Fast-forward 23 years to where, though many things have changed, the fundamental needs of business and the drivers for success have not. Company goals continue to be missed and projects successfully completed and celebrated, but aren't tied in any direct way to the firm's strategy.

On the software development side, lots of clients and colleagues are successfully adopting Agile Software Development practices and are very interested in figuring out how to apply the same principles to other aspects of their business. As we overheard one leader lament, *"We can get our software done right, but why can't management make sure that we are working on the right things?"* We began to realize that what was missing wasn't new tools, processes, techniques or templates, but rather an inclusive framework that laid out how to make strategy execution more agile.

Our intent in this book, is to leverage leading edge thinking and successful practice in the strategy execution space, as well as our over 60 years of collective experience as both practitioners and consultants, to help the reader achieve three key learning outcomes:

- Learn new terms, methodologies and challenges in Agile Strategy Execution.
- Develop an understanding of our Agile Strategy Execution principles, maturity model and framework.
- Highlight best practice tools and solutions to aid in enabling your firm's strategy execution to become more agile.

THE CURRENT STATE OF STRATEGY EXECUTION

In the early to mid-1990s, based on success in the Japanese automotive sector in the 1980s, *Business Reengineering* and *Total Quality Management* were all the rage. Unfortunately, even after millions of dollars were spent, studies showed that on average 67-80% of all TQM programs that were instigated didn't create the desired results and 70% of all reengineering initiatives failed. These concepts in the end, though valuable, were not the *magic bullet* for more effective strategy execution. Fast forward a decade later and unfortunately, not much had changed. A 2002 Information Technology (IT) research study indicated that 80% of major systems development investments either delivered capabilities that were not used or didn't come close to delivering the intended impact. The Standish Group International Inc. has also echoed these sentiments when reporting in 2014 that a *staggering* 31% of IT projects will be canceled before they get completed. Only 9% will likely finish on time and on budget and only 42% will deploy their originally proposed features and functions.

In the mid-2000s, change management was seen as the answer, yet a 2006 global study of 1,500 executives indicated that 62% of change initiatives failed to create the desired performance results. In 2013, a comprehensive study of the opinions of nearly 600 global executives by the Project Management Institute, in conjunction with The Economist's Intelligence Unit, indicated that when assessing the previous three years, respondents felt, on average, that just 56% of their strategic initiatives were successful. For 61%, one of their biggest challenges was in *"bridging the gap between strategy formulation and its day-to-day implementation."* Even those organizations that were classified as *Best Executors,* only delivered a 73% initiative execution success rate. Recent Harvard Business School research, based on the opinions of 400 global CEO's, indicates that executional excellence is still the number one challenge (from a list of 80) facing global leaders. What is more confounding, is that at the same time, 77% of these same managers believed that all their company's strategic priorities have the financial and human resources that are needed for success.

The situation becomes more critical when we start to assess the current employee engagement landscape, which one would think would be highly correlated with effective strategy execution. According to recent Gallup surveys, the state of employee engagement is truly alarming, with only 13% of worldwide employees confirming that they are engaged at work. By this they mean that they *"begin their day with a sense of purpose and finish it with a sense of achievement. They are dedicated to their jobs and engrossed in their roles."* It seems that not only are 65% unengaged, but also another 25% are actively disengaged. Disengaged means that employees *"speak poorly about the company to friends and family, co-worker interactions tilt to the negative and not only do they achieve less, but they have fewer creative moments at work."*

So what is really going on here? As illustrated in the cartoon below, lots of kudos are provided to those who develop new innovative strategies, but few rewards come to those who are accountable for strategy execution. Why is this? Why is effective strategy execution such a challenge? In order to find some answers to this question, we first need to more deeply explore the difference between strategy and execution and what some of the major obstacles are to closing the loop between the two. As Lawrence Hrebiniak, Professor Emeritus with the Department of Management at the University of Pennsylvania's Wharton School so eloquently said, *"It should not be a question of developing strategy and hoping it works, but of developing a strategy and following a logical plan to reach it."*

Peter Drucker, the great-grandfather of management fundamentals, describes strategy as a *"system of values and beliefs, whose ideas shape the whole direction of the company."* According to Michael Porter, another thought-leader in the field of *Competitive Advantage, "the essence of strategy is in choosing what not to do."* Though both of these concepts are fundamentally true, a more Zen-like definition describes strategy as the *"art and science of planning and marshaling resources for their most efficient and effective use in the achievement of a goal or a solution to a problem."*

In other words, strategy is the *connector* between the goals and objectives of the organization and the execution plan, and defines *how* a specific goal is going to be achieved. John Kotter, the renowned founder of the change management movement, puts it another way and believes that *"strategy should be viewed as a dynamic force that constantly seeks opportunities, identifies initiatives that will capitalize on them and completes those initiatives swiftly and efficiently."*

Execution, on the other hand, reflects the carrying out or completion of the steps required to implement a successful strategy. According to The Economist study, *"poor strategic implementation hinders the ability of formal strategy to affect what the firm does in practice."* Let us state that again, *"poor strategic implementation hinders the ability of formal strategy to affect what the firm does in practice."* So what exactly are some of the obstacles, myths and roadblocks hindering effective strategy execution?

OBSTACLES TO EFFECTIVE STRATEGY EXECUTION

Dr. Lawrence Hrebiniak, who authored Making Strategy Work: Leading Effective Execution and Change, has suggested that the number one reason that strategies fail is simply the fact that the *"strategies that are chosen aren't clear or their focus is allowed to shift over time."* His research has shown, and we can certainly attest to the fact, that *"many strategies are just descriptions of aspirational intent with no underlying specific, measurable and time-bound goals that they are supposed to support."* Other key obstacles that Hrebiniak's research has uncovered include:

- The **impact of poor or inadequate cross-functional communications, synchronization and information sharing,** either between the right individuals or between the right business units. More importantly, not enough energy is focused on ensuring that execution plans get communicated to all of the people involved. Often this lack of effective communication results in a lack of a universal feeling of ownership of either the strategy or the execution steps/plans. According to Jeroen De Flander, a European-based strategy execution thought leader and author of 'Strategy Execution Heroes', *"Most of us know the marketing concept of good communication, but to make a message stick in the head of a future consumer, you need to deliver the message seven times using seven different channels. Why do executives think that to make a strategy stick, a boring speech delivered once will be enough?"*
- The **power of existing internal cultural factors and the difficulties involved in managing change effectively**. It is well known that most people start out resistant to change, which can become acute in an organization where there is an

existing power structure with vested interests in keeping things as they are.

- **Executive inattention and lack of rigorous follow through to make sure that the decided upon plans get executed in the time frames expected**. Research by consultant Marakon Associates and the Economist Intelligence Unit of 197 companies also support this view. Their research suggests that fewer than 15% of firms routinely track how their most important execution efforts ACTUALLY perform over how they were EXPECTED to perform. Not surprisingly, these firms achieved only 63% of the expected results of their strategic plans.

MYTHS ABOUT EFFECTIVE STRATEGY EXECUTION

It also turns out that there are all kinds of myths about strategy execution that need to be looked at in a different light. In March 2015, the Harvard Business Review published insights from Donald Sull, Rebecca Homkes and Charles Sull concerning a large-scale project they initiated to identify ways to help complex organizations execute their strategies more effectively. Their research included an analysis of 40 change experiments and survey results from nearly 8,000 managers in more than 250 companies. According to them, Strategy Execution means *"seizing opportunities that support the strategy, while coordinating with other parts of the organization on an ongoing basis."* This means establishing a system that supports not just the finding of *"creative solutions to unforeseen problems,"* but one that also enables the *"running with new unexpected opportunities that appear on the horizon."* One third of all managers surveyed indicate that their organizations react far too slowly or too fast to changing market circumstances and in the process, either lose sight of the company's strategy or are unable to modify the company's strategy in a timely fashion. The specific myths that they debunked were impressive.

- ***Myth #1: Execution equals Alignment:*** Though top-down alignment and cascading of goals is important, another barrier is lack of cross-functional coordination. Their research found that more than 50% of managers want more structure in the processes for coordinating activities across units.
- ***Myth #2: Execution Means Sticking to the Plan:*** Lack of agility is a major obstacle to effective execution. Managers are craving more fluid mechanisms to reallocate funds, people and attention as circumstances change, within a specific set of strategic boundaries.
- ***Myth #3: Communications Equals Understanding:*** The number of communications outputs, including emails, announcements, FAQs or *Meetings-in-a-Box*, is not the same as enabling clear understanding, throughout the organization of a core set of key messages on how a firm's strategy, priorities and initiatives all fit together to drive achievement of a specific set of goals.
- ***Myth #4: A Performance Culture Drives Execution:*** Though past performance measurements are necessary, they aren't sufficient to predict future performance. The internal public and private cultures must be aligned and care about agility, teamwork, and ambition, and be willing to innovate and support experimental failures.
- ***Myth #5: Execution should be Driven Top-Down:*** Effective execution needs to be driven from the middle and guided from the top. In other words, executives should enable more structured processes to facilitate coordination and model teamwork.

STRATEGY EXECUTION ROADBLOCKS

Another interesting perspective presented by Davis, Frechette and Boswell from The Forum Corporation in their 2010 book, Strategic Speed, suggests that one of the major reasons strategy execution is not as effective as it could be is because there is insufficient attention paid to the *human factors*. After exhaustive reviews of hundreds of examples of sluggish and accelerated execution, 18 in-depth case studies of firms that were successfully executing faster than average, and a global survey of 343 senior leaders in fast and not-so-fast firms, they came to the conclusion that too much attention is paid to speed for speed's sake which results in either over attention to *pace* or over attention to *process* when the real key is to reflect on what is truly *adding value*. This added value, they suggest, comes from focusing on three human factors that stand out, namely clarity, unity and agility:

- **CLARITY** means *"making sure that all employees can answer these key questions easily and confidently. Where are we going and why? What are the external conditions we face? What are our internal capabilities? Based on all these factors, what should we do and when should we act?"*
- **UNITY** means *"ensuring that once teams are clear on where they are headed, they agree wholeheartedly on the merits of that direction and the need to work together to move ahead."*
- **AGILITY** means *"heading consistently in a specific direction, but being willing to adapt and course correct as conditions demand and the environment changes."*

In other words, as Davis, Frechette and Boswell wrote, *"You may hire brilliant employees and conceive brilliant strategies, but unless you can reduce the time it takes for employees, leaders, teams or initiatives to contribute to the enterprise in the manner and to the extent that they were meant to contribute and then ensure that they continue to contribute, you won't really be accelerating execution."* Or as Peter Drucker once said, *"There is nothing so useless as doing efficiently that which should not be done at all."*

The net-net is that strategic planning needs to keep up with the times. After years of both practical and consulting experience, we believe that it is time for a new integrated approach to center our thinking. We need to use the best-in-class processes, tools and techniques that have been evolving over the last few years. We need to pivot our thinking to one that encourages organizations to cultivate continuous course corrections based on digitized actionable intelligence resulting from the realities encountered in their competitive landscape. To do so, both people and processes need to take advantage of new digitization developments such as collaboration platforms, digital experience-based workflow, project, program and portfolio management automation, anchored by an agile strategy execution process that drives engaged, coordinated and responsive decision-making. In the next chapter, we'll discuss what we are seeing as the missing links for agile strategy execution.

AGILE STRATEGY EXECUTION

This idea of enabling execution agility is not exactly new and for the last 15+ years has been a key driver behind finding better ways for developing software that can respond to change. Originally published in 2001 as part of what was then called the *Agile Manifesto* were four main points, which at the time were quite revolutionary, namely the value of:

- Individuals and interactions over processes and tools.
- Working software through proven incremental improvements over comprehensive specifications, business

requirements and other documentation.

- Focusing on customer collaboration over contract negotiation.
- Responding to change over rigidly following a plan.

Since then, Agile Software Development, supported and promoted by such organizations as the Scrum Alliance (www.scrumalliance.org) and the Agile Alliance (www.agilealliance.org) has become a fundamental business practice based on the idea that *"solutions evolve through collaboration between self-organizing, cross-functional teams utilizing the appropriate practices for their context."* Central to this concept are twelve key principles, outlined by the Agile Alliance (www.agilealliance.org) that we have consolidated into seven concepts that we believe reflect the core philosophy needed for true business agility, namely:

- Satisfy through early and continuous delivery of value as simply as possible while welcoming and harnessing change for competitive advantage.
- Deliver results frequently with a preference for shorter timescales, with results being the primary measure of progress.
- Ensure that cross-functional teams work together frequently throughout, with the most efficient and effective communication method being face-to-face conversation.
- Build work around motivated individuals and self-organizing teams. Give them the environment and support they need, and trust them to get the job done.
- Promote sustainable work efforts so that teams can maintain a constant pace indefinitely.
- Continuously pay attention to excellence and good design.

- At regular intervals, ensure that the team reflects on how to become more effective, then tunes and adjusts behavior accordingly.

Another important agility tenet is the idea of *scrum theory,* which according to The Scrum Guide, developed and sustained by Ken Schwaber and Jeff Sutherland, posits that *"knowledge comes from experience"* and that decision-making should assess what is known using an iterative, incremental approach based on:

- *"Transparency and a common understanding of what is being seen.*
- *Inspection of results with the ability to assess and detect undesirable variances.*
- *Adaptability and effective course corrections when results deviate from expected tolerances."*

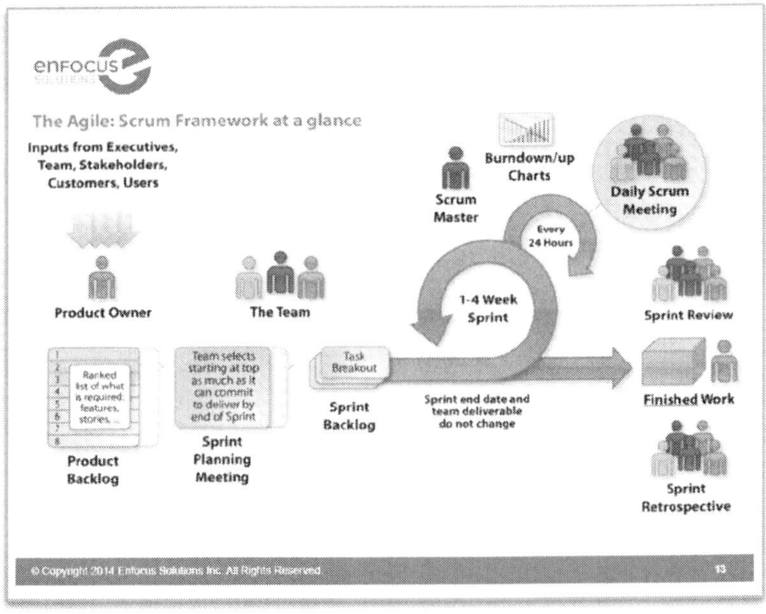

As outlined in the figure on the previous page from John E. Parker of enFOCUS Solutions Inc., *Scrum Theory* involves the translation of inputs from users, executives, customers, stakeholders etc. into a set of *user stories*, each of which represents a specific feature or requirement that are grouped into *epics* resulting in a prioritized *backlog* of what is needed to be accomplished. Teams then organize 1-to-4-week work efforts or *sprints*, during which they try to convert as many user stories as they can into usable, actionable software code. The sprints are anchored by daily face-to-face *scrum meetings* where everyone reports on what they accomplished the previous day, what they intend to do that day, share lessons learned and seek support from team members to resolve issues and roadblocks. These pieces are then reviewed with *end users* and once approved, are assembled into *finished work*, which is then released in an organized fashion. Periodic team *retrospectives* are held to reflect on what's working, what's not, what new strengths are needed, set priorities if needed and what can be done to improve *Time to Value*.

In addition to leveraging some of the core *Agile Manifesto* and *Scrum Theory* principles, our Agile Strategy Execution Framework™ also builds upon the collective work of many other strategy and execution methodologies and practices including Lean, Six Sigma, Kaizen, Systems Thinking, Business Digitization, Collaboration Platforms as well as new developments in organization innovation and DevOps. For those unaware, DevOps, according to Wikipedia, is a *"new cultural shift based on collaboration between software development, operations and testing organizations*."

STRATEGY EXECUTION'S MISSING LINKS

For most strategy practitioners, strategy execution at its core is a term used to *"describe the activities within an organization to manage the execution of a strategic plan."* Larry Bossidy, former CEO of Allied Signal and Ram Charan, who wrote **Execution: The Discipline of Getting Things Done,** take it one step further and suggest that strategy execution is a *"systematic way of exposing reality and acting on it."* We have taken these two definitions and would like to propose that AGILE strategy execution means *"translating strategy into a reality that is aligned, accountable and responsive."*

If strategy execution is **ALIGNED**, it means that all components of strategy (goals and objectives, strategic priorities, and initiative investment portfolios) are linked and coordinated. Processes exist to coordinate all departments or areas both vertically and horizontally. All Run-the-Business (RTB) activities, tactics and other strategic programs or projects must cascade from the linked objectives to functional or cross-functional teams.

If an organization, function or team is **ACCOUNTABLE**, it means that all employees involved in strategy execution are committed to what is being created with direct and visible line of sight to goals and strategy. They can see clearly the interconnectedness as well as their role and value contribution. In other words, they are data and outcome-driven with strong group buy-in to ongoing processes for regularly measuring, assessing and reporting *progress to plan*. Any metric variances lead to real-time discussion and refinements of team plans, budgets and actions.

If the strategy execution process is **RESPONSIVE**, it means that there is in place a culture and governance process that supports ongoing adaptation and realignment to evolving or changing internal and external landscapes. Cross department objectives, projects, actions and metrics are managed real-time in a way that results in frequent and ongoing plan and activity discussions and decision-making processes based on data-driven critical assessments of performance with public views and common definitions of all measurements and analytical processes.

In other words, **Agile Strategy Execution** delivers timely value in an aligned, accountable and responsive way that contributes to the achievement of identified goals or business outcomes. These include growing revenue, improved margins through more effective internal processes, strengthened customer satisfaction, loyalty and intimacy, risk reduction and driving competitive advantage.

Each of these three pillars (Alignment, Accountability and Responsiveness) is supported by a set of *Best Practices* and in many cases new digital (real-time) solutions that push the industry in some new directions and force us to pivot our way of thinking. In the next chapter we'll share in more detail this Agile Strategy Execution Framework™. But before we do, here are a few last thoughts. One inquiry that often comes up is to ask why a strategy execution framework is even necessary. What we have seen is that there is today this plethora of tools, methods, processes and enablers both in literature and practice. But there is little that provides practical advice as to how to compile all of these *best-in-class* approaches so that they can be easily deployed in a holistic way. Our intent is two-fold. Firstly, is to give the strategy-execution practitioner a systematic and workable way to approach, communicate, align and deploy the use of all of these various processes, methods and tools. Secondly, is to provide an agile strategy execution maturity model that helps organizations assess their own progress in executing strategy with more agility on an evolving scale and ascertain where they would like to be in the future. In both scenarios, our Agile Strategy Execution Framework™ can be used to target improvement areas and provide guideposts and methods as to how to move up the maturity curve.

FINDING TRUE NORTH AND CONNECTING THE DOTS

Also central to our perspective is the idea that in order to enable this *pivot* in thinking towards a more agile view of strategy execution and *Connect the Dots*, it is critical that organizations and departments understand clearly where they are today and where they would like to be in the future. As Alice in Wonderland author, Lewis Carroll, wrote, *"If you don't know where you are going, any road will take you there!"* Specifically, this means assessing each of our three key Agile Strategy Execution pillars (Alignment, Accountability and Responsiveness) along a multi-phased evolution curve. There are four stages in this evolution curve, namely Task Oriented, Managed Oriented, Integrated Oriented and Optimized Oriented.

Each of these stages has a set of strategy execution parameters, including such processes as a review of who is involved with the planning process, what tools and techniques support it, how are strategic investments made and lastly an assessment of the depth and breadth of cross-functional stakeholder involvement. Additional details as to the meaning of each of these parameters in each of the four stages are discussed in more depth in the Techniques Appendix. On the next page is a high-level summary to provide readers with a sense of what we are talking about.

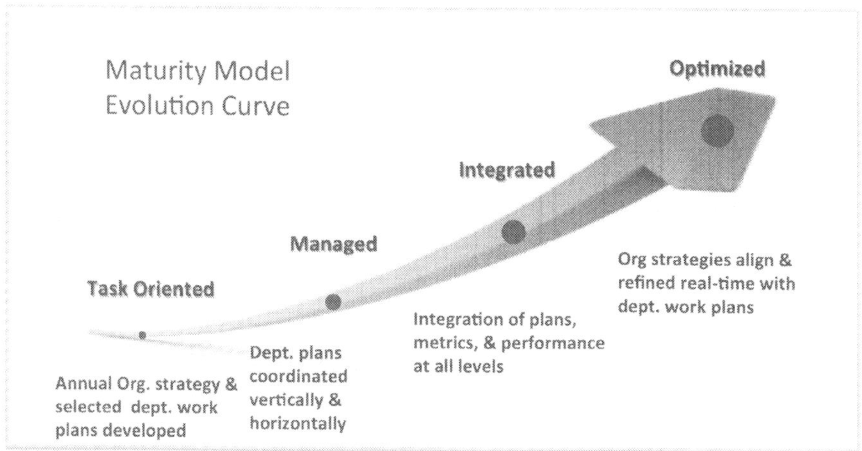

The most important concept to remember at this point is that the use of this maturity model enables an organization to assess where they are today in the strategy execution process, and then use our Agile Strategy Execution Framework™ to target areas that need improvement accordingly.

THE AGILE STRATEGY EXECUTION FRAMEWORK™

Now that you have a pretty good understanding of the basics of some *Agile Concepts*, and our Agile Strategy Execution Maturity Model™, it's time to introduce our Agile Strategy Execution Framework™. We call it a framework because it's not a step-by-step process but rather a set of attributes or dimensions that define a truly agile strategy execution ecosystem. Any dimension can be worked on at any time using a wide variety of *best-in-class* tools, techniques, processes and applications.

However, before we begin, we need to clarify some assumptions that we are making that are an integral part of effective deployment of our Agile Strategy Execution Framework™.

- Firstly, we are assuming that you have in place a well-articulated strategic plan that outlines the organization's value proposition and vision, it's mission or charter with key goals that are S.M.A.R.T. i.e. specific, measurable, achievable, relevant and time-bound.

- Secondly, we are assuming that these S.M.A.R.T. goals have been translated into specific strategies that are in turn translated into funded execution priorities, which can be projects, programs, process improvement efforts or run-the-business activities.
- Thirdly, we are assuming that all tactical projects, programs and important work efforts are tied to the strategy in some way, regardless of whether or not they are grouped into actual or virtual portfolios of various kinds or managed through PMO's. (Program or Portfolio Management Offices)
- Fourthly, is the assumption that all key business plan assumptions have been articulated and documented and are well understood by the leadership team. At a minimum, these business plan assumptions should cover internal and external topics. Internal topics should include areas such as budget availability over time, expected revenue growth forecasts, talent availability and business model stability. External topics should include such areas as market opportunity and competitor positioning or technology, social, economic or political trends.

As an example of the kinds of assumptions that should be documented, the large high tech firm, whose story we shared in the prologue, had a strategy to move a large percentage of its business to a new recurring revenue-based operating model within 18 months. Some of the internal assumptions that needed to be documented included revenue growth projections, expected time frames to adoption, expectations as to the ease of creating and filling new roles and the potential level of resistance to such a culture change. External factors that needed to be considered included the speed of customer adoption of cloud-consumption subscription-based operating models, and of course, competitor reactions. Funded execution priorities included a number of program tracks across each selling motion (Land, Adopt & Expand and Renew):

- Documenting, selling motion playbook sales engagement strategies.
- Establishing a number of new roles with requisite training and career paths.
- Building a new digital experience-based marketing demand-gen practice.
- Implementing new channel and outsource partnering strategies and incentives.
- Defining new services offers along with back-office systems and IT changes.

As mentioned previously, strategy execution becomes agile by using agile concepts to drive alignment, accountability and responsiveness. As a reminder, if strategy execution is ALIGNED, it means that all components of strategy (goals and objectives, strategic priorities, and initiative investment portfolios) are linked and coordinated both vertically and horizontally. If an organization, function or team is ACCOUNTABLE, it means that all employees involved in strategy execution are committed to what is being created with direct and visible line of sight, and can see clearly the interconnectedness i.e. their role and value contribution. If the strategy execution process is RESPONSIVE, it means that there is in place a culture and governance process that supports ongoing adaptation and realignment to evolving or changing internal and external landscapes.

Traditionally, most organizations executed strategy through the use of *strategy cascades* that generally looked like the next figure. Company goals flowed through the organization in a *waterfall* with reports generated at each level. The challenge, as we all know with waterfalls, is that trying to push the water back up the river is really difficult, especially when there are few effective processes or mechanisms to do so and in spite of a multitude of *open door* management policies and practices.

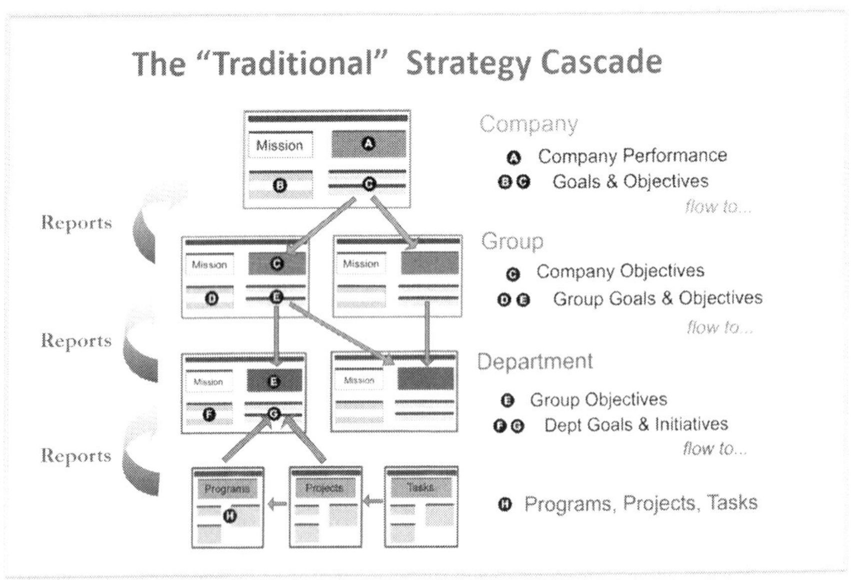

Our Agile Strategy Execution Framework™ is composed of six *Dimensions* and two *Influencing Factors*, which we'll summarize now, and then, review each in detail in the next chapter.

Dimension #1: Detailed Plans and Metrics: This involves incorporating a systematic and disciplined approach that focuses on translating breakthrough organizational goals, objectives and strategies into specific functional area, team and individual plans and their associated metrics.

Dimension #2: Align and Link: This dimension means ensuring that strategic goals are aligned and linked to projects, programs, run-the-business activities and process improvement efforts both vertically and cross-functionally at all organization levels. A crucial element is *catch-ball,* a process whereby stakeholder inputs and refinements are proactively encouraged up and down and across as part of the aligning and linking process.

Dimension #3: Real-Time Updates: The Real-Time Updates dimension involves enabling a firm-wide, online, transparent, *Single Source of Truth* for all plan collaboration, engagement and reporting. It then involves driving real-time plan updates based on day-to-day *triggers* so as to ensure properly prioritized and scheduled work.

Dimension #4: Cadence Decisions: In this dimension, different action meetings occur at multiple levels of the organization with the objective of ensuring proactive real-time resourcing, course correction solutioning, and backlog management decision-making processes.

Dimension #5: Innovation Bets: Innovation Bets involve identifying and executing small opportunities to study, pilot or test new innovations that reflect current market conditions, new technology or other advances.

Dimension #6: Refresh or Transform: This last dimension involves formally reassessing core business assumptions, updating strategic plans or tactics, reviewing priorities, linkages and alignment and then *pivoting* as needed.

Influencing Factor #1 Culture Impacts: The culture Influencing Factor involves assessing formal vs. informal, and preached vs. practiced corporate culture norms. Leaders can then either use their culture as an enabling driver for managing change or if needed initiate processes to drive needed culture change.

Influencing Factor #2 Connected Governance™: The Connected Governance™ Influencing Factor involves connecting leadership practices, employee engagement mechanisms and collaboration processes using leading edge digitization experiences to provide actionable intelligence.

Assessing these Dimensions and the impacts of the Influencing Factors as enabling or disabling forces are critical for agility and effective business strategy course correction, especially in an era of the *Internet of Things* and advanced digitization. The benefits of such an approach are that:

- It is inclusive and can be used with all best practice tools and techniques used by organizations today.
- It is strict in intent, yet flexible in delivery style.
- Success can be measured, showing before and after results.
- Each dimension can be worked on separately or together, in whatever order is best for the organization.

DIMENSIONS OF THE AGILE STRATEGY EXECUTION ™

Let's now review each of these dimensions in detail, first by providing some context, illustrating with current *Best Practices*, providing some actual success examples and then sharing key outcomes and benefits.

DETAILED PLANS AND METRICS

As indicated above, *Detailed Plans and Metrics* involves incorporating a systematic and disciplined approach that focuses on translating organizational S.M.A.R.T goals, objectives, strategies and execution priorities into breakthrough initiative or *Run-the-Business* functional area plans and their associated *Key Performance Indicators* (KPIs). There exist all sorts of different models that can be used to engage teams. Some of the most popular, that we've summarized on the next few pages, are Hoshin Kanri Planning or Policy Deployment, OGSM – (Objectives, Goals, Strategy, Metrics) OKR – Objectives and Key Results and the Balanced Scorecard.

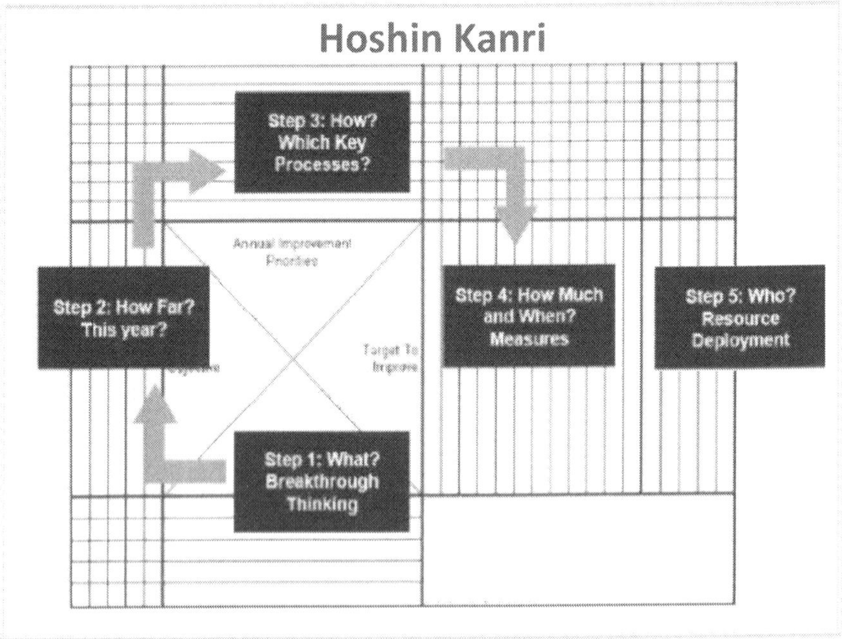

This methodology originated in Japan and generally translates into the *management of methodology for setting strategic direction*. It's a top-down process whereby top management-defined vision, high-level goals and strategies are translated downward through the organization with the strategy at the highest level becoming the achievement goal for the next level down. It's designed to ensure that high-level insight and vision remain *alive and well* after the planning process is over and that the long-range plan doesn't end up on a shelf or become a doorstop. Teams at each level participate in deciding on the strategy, setting the appropriate targets, creating the detailed action plans and determining the relevant metrics to achieve their level's goals. Teams and levels communicate with each other using what is called a *catch-ball* technique, whereby the proposed plans are shared and input welcomed in such a way that it ensures buy-in from everyone in the organization. Once the plan is agreed to, the leaders at each level in the organization drive regular reviews of progress, resolve issues and decide on corrective action where appropriate. The focus is on getting clarity between where you are and where you want to be, having a realistic assessment of what execution resources exist and prioritizing in such a way that only a few priorities are worked on. The rest should be placed in *backlog*, to be considered later as circumstances allow or change. Alas, in many companies, priority setting often means *can't ever do* and backlog ideas and projects are lost unless picked up as unofficial or under the radar skunk projects.

OGSM (OBJECTIVES, GOALS, STRATEGY, METRICS)

OGSM is another strategy formulation and communication tool that also has roots in Japan, in the automotive industry. The big difference here is the need to clarify the way in which Objectives are different from Goals. An objective, from the perspective of the OGSM model, must be a statement that reflects ultimately what the organization wants to achieve that is breakthrough, specific and possible. Goals, on the other hand, translate the objective into some sort of numeric, binary, traceable clarification that serves as a sort of stepping stone to the achievement of the objective and must be Specific-Measurable-Achievable and Compatible. Strategy in this model reflects focus. In other words, how and where resources are going to be applied to achieve the objectives and goals. Like goals, strategies need to be specific, drive differentiation and be written in such a way that NOT doing them is not a respectable option.

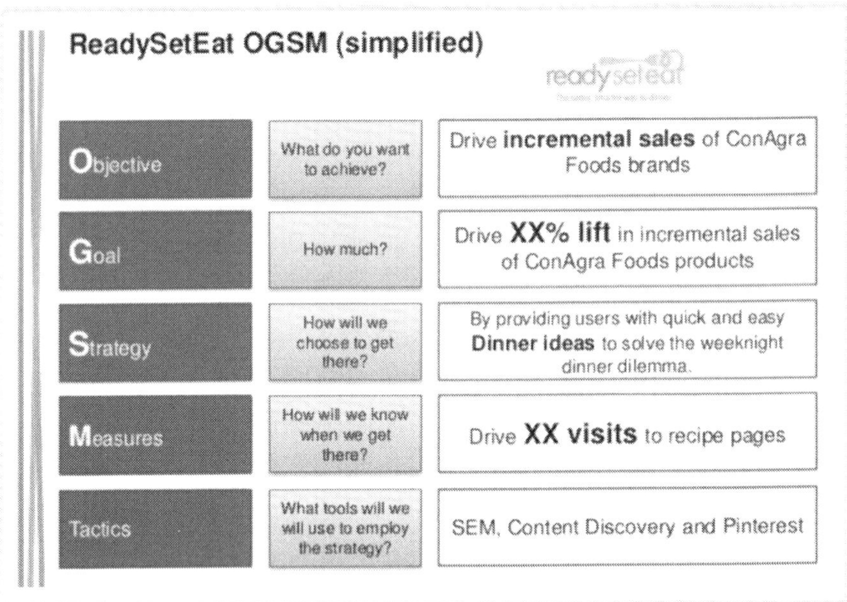

For example, suggesting that the organization *drive operational excellence and quality* is not an effective strategy because no organization would proactively choose to operate badly and/or with poor quality. It's also helpful if the strategy statement makes it clear what the organization is not going to focus on. For many firms, this process is extremely difficult. As Davis, Frechette and Boswell from The Forum Corporation have shared, *"often strategies and initiative objectives are stated at such a high level that it's difficult to identify projects that don't align, thereby making it difficult to determine what to say 'NO' to."* Performance metrics also need to be specific, measurable, achievable and compatible. They also need to be numeric and traceable with a single owner who is accountable to deliver the results required by the strategy. In summary, under the OGSM model, objectives and goals reflect *what* the organization wants to do and strategy and metrics reflect *how* the organization will execute.

OKR – OBJECTIVES AND KEY RESULTS

OKR is a model that venture capitalist John Doerr, a partner at Kleiner, Perkins, Caufield and Byers, brought over from Intel to Google and is now used at firms such as LinkedIn, Sears, Zynga, Oracle and Twitter. The general idea is that objectives should be ambitious and a little outside of the organization, function, team or personal comfort zone. Each objective should have 2-4 measurable results, which must be *"quantifiable, and clearly make the objective achievable and lead to objective grading"* on some sort of scale such as 0-1.0, as Google uses, or 1-100%. As Doerr articulated in his original 1999 presentation on the subject:

"Personal OKR's define what the person is working on. Team OKR's define priorities for the whole team, and are not just a collection of all individual OKRs. Company OKR's are big picture and articulate the top-level focus for the entire company."

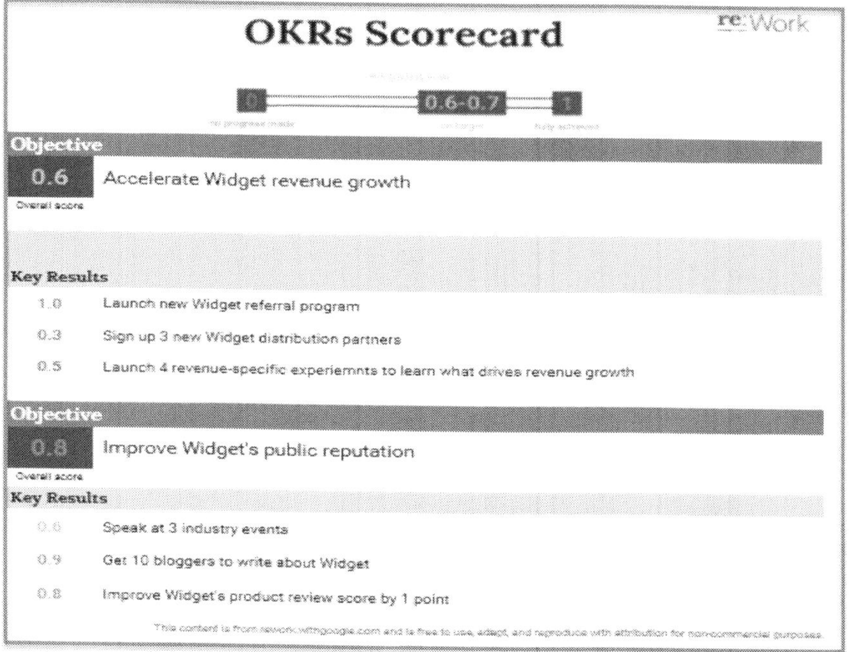

No individual should have more than 3-5 objectives and they should be achievable within a specific quarter and checked with a reasonable degree of frequency. They also should be publicly available so that everyone at any level in the organization can collectively see the OKR's and their progress. Some organizations review OKR's at the individual or team level weekly, others do so on a monthly basis. Any corporate OKR's should be reviewed at a minimum quarterly. Most should be operational in nature, but some can be aspirational, what Google calls *Moonshots*. The expectation is that the execution strategy and tactics needed to enable achievement are articulated, so that the individual and the team understand clearly which activity enabled the desired results. There is also a focus, when results aren't achieved, to better understand why. This helps the team discuss what can be done to ensure that better results can be achieved the next time or ascertain whether nor not the objective needs to pivot so as to be perhaps more realistic.

DASHBOARDS AND THE BALANCED SCORECARD

Originally popularized by Kaplan and Norton in the mid-1990s, The Balanced Scorecard is another strategy performance management tool that was built on the idea that in order to ensure long-term success, an organization must develop goals and metrics based on more than just financial measures.

In order to be *balanced*, the organization should also consider three other business aspects including, Customer (How do customers see us?), Internal Process (What must we excel at from a business process perspective?) and Learning and Growth (How can we continue to improve, create value and innovate?). On the next page is an example of a typical Balanced Scorecard structure.

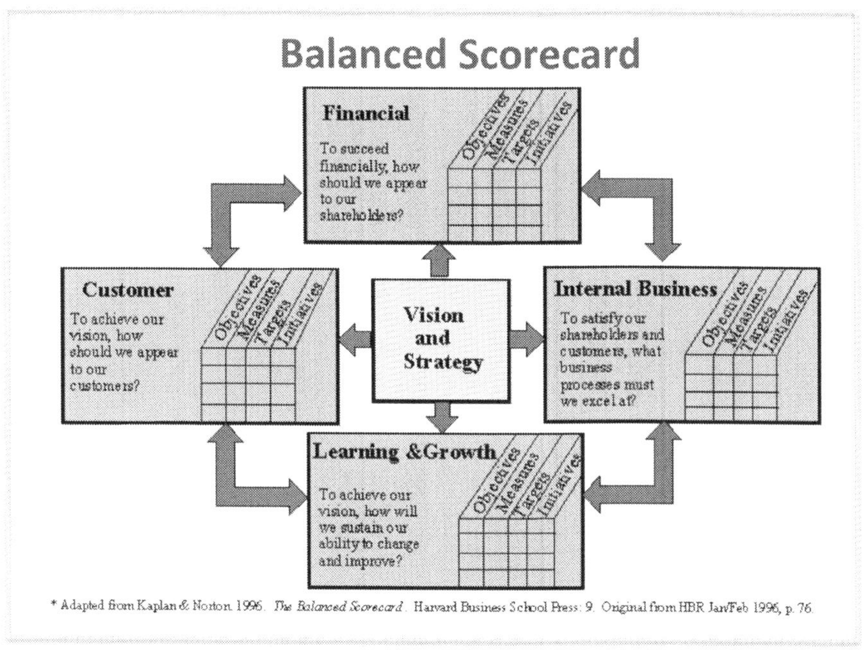

DETAILED PLANS AND METRIC SUCCESS EXAMPLES

Below and on the next page are several examples of various kinds of analog and digital dashboards. The first example shows a typical

Balanced Scorecard Example

FINANCIAL			FY11			
Metric Name	**Functional Owner**	**Target**	**Q1**	**Q2**	**Q3**	**Q4**
Costs per Person Housed (Costs/PH)	Delivery	<=14,717 Q1<=14,533 Q2<=14,348 Q3<=14,164 Q	$ 14,449	$ 13,434	$ 13,116	
Costs per Square Foot (Costs/SF)	Delivery	<=50 Q1<=50 Q2<=51 Q3<=51 Q4	$ 50	$ 46	$ 46	
Operational Variance	Delivery & Finance	>=0%, <=2%	2.0%	0.4%	1.0%	
Capital in Service Variance	Delivery & Finance	>=0%, <=10%	[illegible]	0.3%	[illegible]	
CLIENT			FY11			
Metric Name	**Functional Owner**	**Target**	**Q1**	**Q2**	**Q3**	**Q4**
Overall Client Satisfaction	Exec	>=3.89	[illegible]	[illegible]	[illegible]	
Client Partnership	Strategy & Planning	>=3.49	[illegible]	[illegible]	[illegible]	
Business Review	Strategy & Planning	>=20% Q1>=40% Q2>=60% Q3>=80% Q4	29%	43%	62%	
Service Request Satisfaction	Delivery	>=4	NA	NA	NA	
PROCESS			FY11			
Metric Name	**Functional Owner**	**Target**	**Q1**	**Q2**	**Q3**	**Q4**
Work Space Utilization	Strategy & Planning	>=51.0% Q1>=51.5% Q2>=52.0% Q3>=52.6% Q4	54%	51.7%	53.6%	
Global Site Strategy (GSS) Alignment	Strategy & Planning	>=91%	100%	100%	100%	
Service Requests & Preventative Mainten	Delivery	>=95.5%	99%	99.7%	98.7%	
Project Delivery	Delivery	>=90%	86%	100%	100%	
Connected Workplace	Solutions	>=9.8% Q1>=10.3% Q2>=10.8% Q3>=11.2% Q4	10%	11.3%	16.43%	
Square Feet per Person Housed (SF/PH)	Strategy & Planning	<=282 Q1<=280 Q2<=277 Q3<=275 Q4	274	284	278	
LEARNING AND GROWTH			FY11			
Metric Name	**Functional Owner**	**Target**	**Q1**	**Q2**	**Q3**	**Q4**
Employee Engagement	Exec	83%	83%	83%	83%	
Development Planning	Exec	73%	70%	70%	80%	
Career Development-40	Exec	>=24% Q1>=48% Q2>=71% Q3>=95% Q4	28%	68%	92%	

Balanced Scorecard where the variances from expected targets are highlighted in a red-yellow-green format. Below, is a personal dashboard that illustrates a detailed plan summary and project effort status and due dates, deliverables and metrics as well as information on meetings, action logs and reports created. In this case, the agreed upon corporate taxonomy is to focus on *Objectives, Initiatives and Actions.* For each component, the status, the owner, current progress and metrics are tracked. For those interested in detailed project plans or charters, there are hyperlinks available to connect the user to the relevant data sources, hopefully online, and not PowerPoint presentations. In the middle is the agreed upon metrics scoreboard. Note that what brings this example *alive,* i.e. real-time, is that there is a field where senior executives are expected to comment on progress or ask questions.

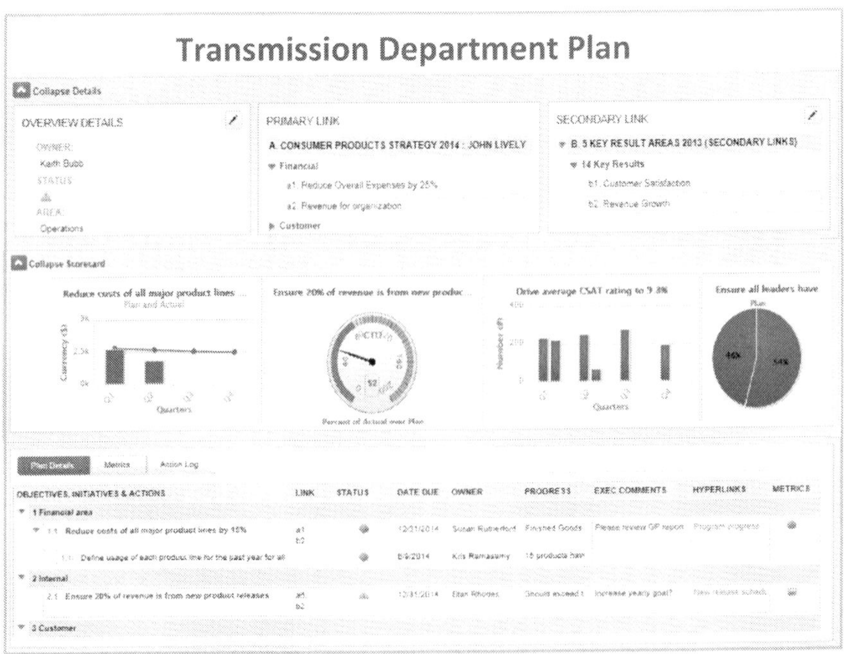

BENEFITS OF DETAILED PLANS AND METRICS

This process of enabling highly transparent plans and metrics throughout the organization leads to a number of critically important outcomes including:

- A transparent Single Source of Truth (SSOT).
- A proactive mechanism that ensures that the firm's strategic goals drive progress and actions at every organizational level.
- Employee involvement through the setting of personal and team targets, improvement schedules and reviews.
- Improved clarity of intent that is S.M.A.R.T. (i.e. Specific, Measurable, Achievable, Results-Focused and Time-Bound). Metrics are directly tied with baselines, targets and variances that are measured & reviewed continuously.
- The right level of connection to the details concerning key programs, projects and their execution tactics.

ALIGN AND LINK

The Align and Link dimension refers to a process that ensures that the strategic goals are properly aligned and linked both vertically and cross-functionally throughout the organization. Primary links connect organizational and departmental plans. Secondary links connect specific plans to other related plans in other organizations. In the case of the large networking organization, the desire to launch a new organization required support from Finance, Human Resources, Sales, Product Management, Marketing, Partner Engagement and the IT departments with the plans for all seven organizations aligned and linked proactively.

There are a number of methods that can be used to drive the alignment and linkage process including, relevancy assessments (whereby teams review the high-level goals and discuss how what they are doing is relevant to the overall goal achievement), performance outcomes mapping exercises, dependency assessments and integrated risk reviews, to name a few. Either way, the critical point is to identify issues between departments and teams, and to enable useful interactions no matter what the process. The most effective engagement process that we have seen so far is an adaptation of the Hoshin Kanri *catch-ball* process. *Catch*

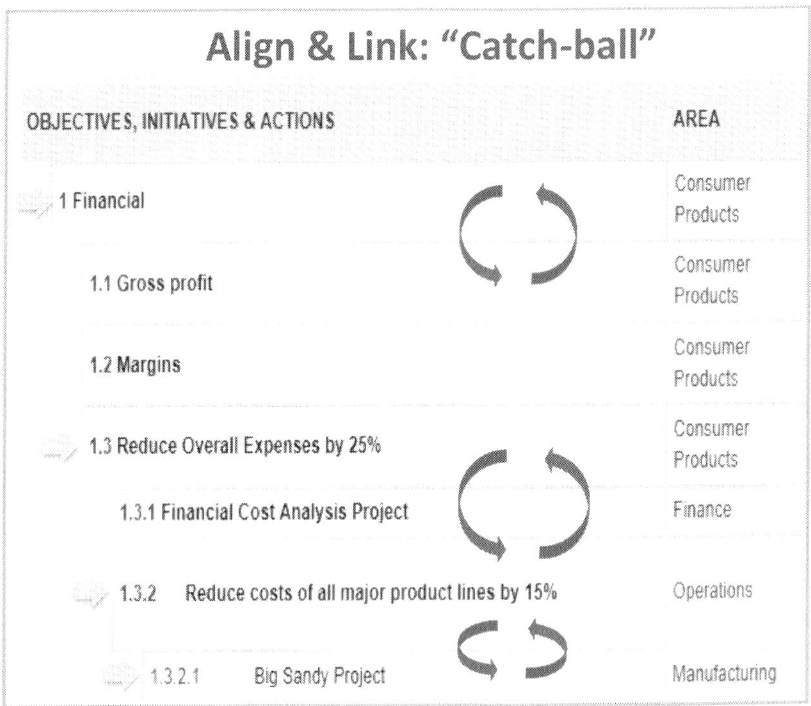

-ball is designed to allow meaningful two-way conversations between employees at all levels and departments of an organization. This ongoing dialog allows for the communication and understanding of not only the intent of the initiatives and strategies, but also of any obstacles and/or methods of making a smoother execution process.

In the example on the previous page, the catch-ball process enables dialogue between the Manufacturing Area, that has responsibility for the Big Sandy project and the Operations Area, which has a goal of reducing costs of all major project lines by 15%. These discussions will help *ALIGN* both the expectations of Operations and help define the scope and deliverables needed for the *LINKED* Big Sandy project. This discussion's results could then generate more conversation and possible refinement of impacted upstream goals.

ALIGN AND LINK SUCCESS EXAMPLES

The example below shows alignment detail where the balanced scorecard is used as the primary plan approach. There are a number of different departments that participate in helping to achieve the goal of 'Reducing Overall Expenses by 25%'. Finance owns the Financial Cost Analysis Project. The Operations Team owns a variety of efforts (both projects and RTB process improvement activities), one of which is the Big Sandy Project in Manufacturing. For each one, current status, progress, metrics and accountability are clearly defined and tracked. What are also visible, in this illustration are

Balanced Scorecard Alignment Detail

OBJECTIVES, INITIATIVES & ACTIONS	AREA	CURRENT QUARTER	METRICS	DATE DUE	OWNER	PROGRESS
1 Financial	Consumer Products			12/31/2014	Matt Gardner	
1.1 Gross profit	Consumer Products			12/31/2014	John Lively	why is this behind schedule
1.2 Margins	Consumer Products			12/31/2014	Paul Garst	
1.3 Reduce Overall Expenses by 25%	Consumer Products			12/31/2014	Joel Welde	Are expenses within target as planne
1.3.1 Financial Cost Analysis Project	Finance			12/31/2014	Jim Carr	Dwight not up to speed yet
1.3.2 Reduce costs of all major product lines by 15%	Operations			12/31/2014	Susan Rutherford	Please review GP report for Marento
1.3.2.1 Big Sandy Project	Manufacturing			5/14/2014	Laurie Bacopoulos	All deliverables on on track
2 Customer	Consumer Products			12/31/2014	Matt Gardner	

TASK	STATUS	% COMPLETE	OWNER	START	PLANNED END
General		0	Laurie Bacopoulos	1/4/2014	2/4/2014
Define		0	Laurie Bacopoulos	2/5/2014	3/5/2014
Measure		0	Laurie Bacopoulos	4/5/2014	5/6/2014

the primary and secondary links. Primary links drive vertical alignment as every team with their projects and Run-the-Business activities are linked to a team above it and that team is linked to the one above it all the way to the top of the organization. Secondary links illustrate all of the known cross function or cross department connections. This brings to light (in addition to duplication of effort) work efforts that are either dependent on or are required inputs from and for other teams.

Below is an example of what the output of an Align and Link end product might look like in an organization chart type view.

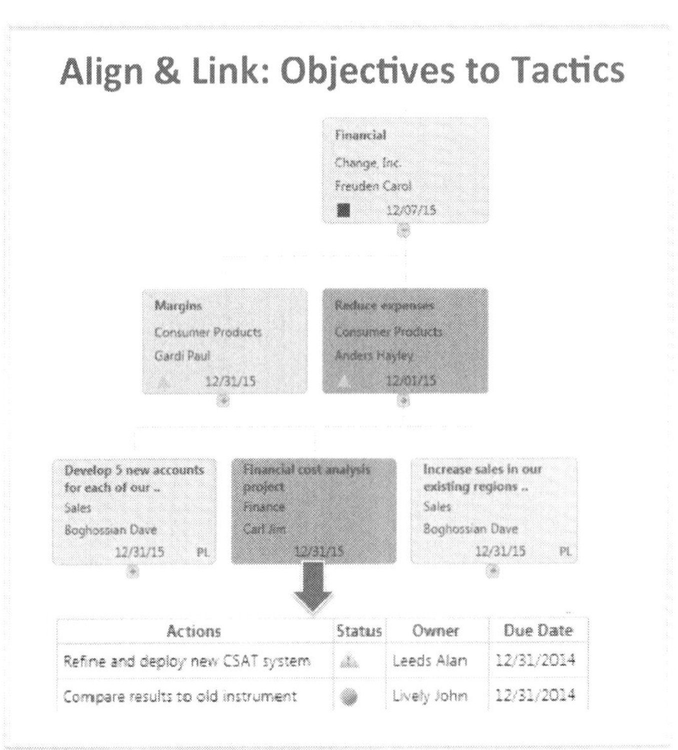

Executives (seeing goals) and project managers (seeing their linked projects and tasks) have a real-time view of status and progress (box and symbol colors) that drives discussion and corrective action.

One interesting story comes from Larry Bossidy, the former CEO of Allied Signal and leader of the movement that views execution as a process. He often managed by *wandering around* and would ask operational team members that he met what the corporate strategy was and how their role aligned and linked with it. If they couldn't answer effectively, he sent them home. He only had to do it a few times before the message got through to all managers and virtual team leaders that this process mattered.

BENEFITS OF ALIGNING AND LINKING:

Effective aligning and linking has a number of really important benefits:

- Firstly, is the establishment of a common language and taxonomy to describe strategic and operational intent.
- Secondly, is the fact that the organization's fundamental organizing concepts can be applied universally, whether it be by channel, by geography or by department - to name a few approaches that we have seen. With real-time transparency, they can be realigned as the organization evolves along a centralized to decentralized pendulum.
- Thirdly, is the establishment of a new set of workable horizontal and vertical feedback loops, as well as clarity and insight into team, program and project interdependencies and issues. Effective alignment and linkage also tend to drive more seamless communication at the right levels and reduce the number of surprises as execution unfolds.
- Fourthly, the establishment of clear line of sight between goals, metrics and resources across all levels and functions helps identify duplication of effort and unsupported initiatives, i.e. those that seem to be *outside the plan*.

- Lastly, clear alignment and linkage enables over time the decentralization of decision-making deeper into the organization based on trust and transparency.

One classic story that illustrates the challenges associated with unsupported initiatives involves a leading computer manufacturer who, as a result of an effective alignment mapping process, discovered that they had over a dozen different teams building user interfaces, which they were able to consolidate into two key efforts that everyone could support. Another involved a large personal computer vendor who discovered that they had sixteen product development teams competing for five available slots in their manufacturing supply chain. Again, it was transparency that enabled the right prioritization and resourcing decision-making.

For our Mid-West Power Supplier's head of Strategy and Planning, the key drivers and benefits of better alignment and linkage were:

- Stronger alignment between business unit work plans and corporate strategic plan
- Enhanced accountability with a stronger line of sight created
- Better tools to facilitate planning process

In order to do so, they made the decision to use an enterprise strategy and planning software solution from Y-Change. This process first involved establishing an agreed upon cross-functional plan hierarchy of work goals and key actions for the four levels of their business, from the corporate strategic plan, to business unit strategic plan, to the business unit work plans, to the department and plant work plans. Accountability emerged through a process of assigning *owners* with named applicable support resources and beginning and end dates to each plan element. Open and transparent access to the same information by all participants was enabled. Primary and secondary links were established among all teams to proactively connect the plans to the strategy. Each area plan, work goal and action was evaluated and assigned a red-yellow-green status along with plan specific KPIs. All of this information was then compiled into various online summary reports for board level approval of work plans and budgets and executive-level reports that provided the capability for Business Unit and Plant VP's and their staffs to select progress and KPI updates.

REAL - TIME UPDATES

The third attribute of our Agile Strategy Execution Framework™, Real-Time Updates, involves institutionalizing a digital, transparent *Single Source of Truth* for all reporting and then driving real-time plan updates based on day-to-day *triggers*. By enabling real-time digital updates for all initiatives, objectives, projects and tactics, collaboration with others regarding priorities and issues becomes a given. In addition, formalized, required deadlines tend to drive meetings with *self* to refine individual team member action plans and backlog priorities. It also encourages appropriate proactive rather than reactive processes for issues escalation and resolution. Every team, function and potentially the whole organization can ensure that resources are properly assigned, and work is properly scheduled and prioritized.

REAL-TIME UPDATES EXAMPLES

On the next page are two screenshots of actual real-time input and scorecard screens. The first one shows Lois' status dashboard for all of the initiatives and projects that she is accountable for. It shows which tasks are due this quarter and need addressing, as well as the

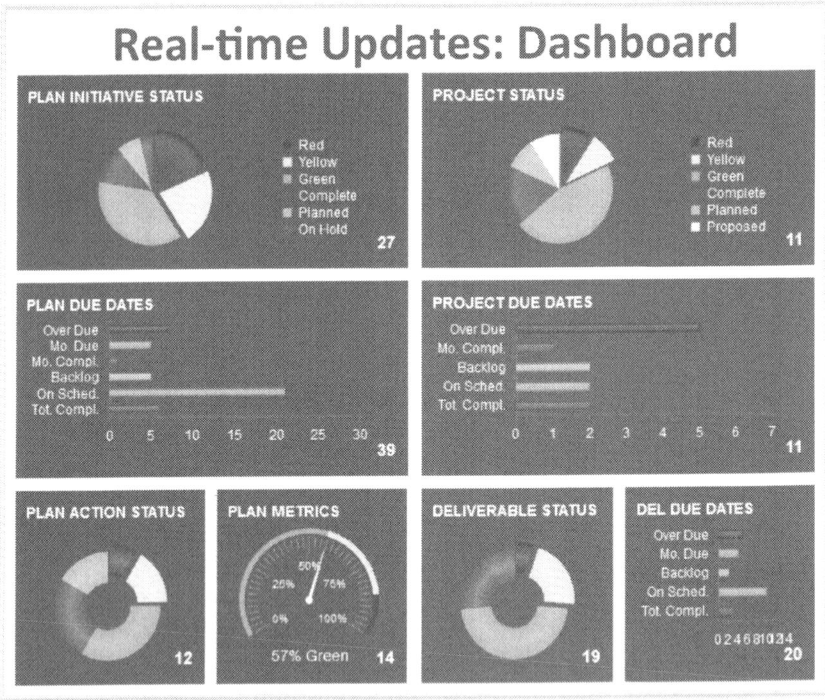

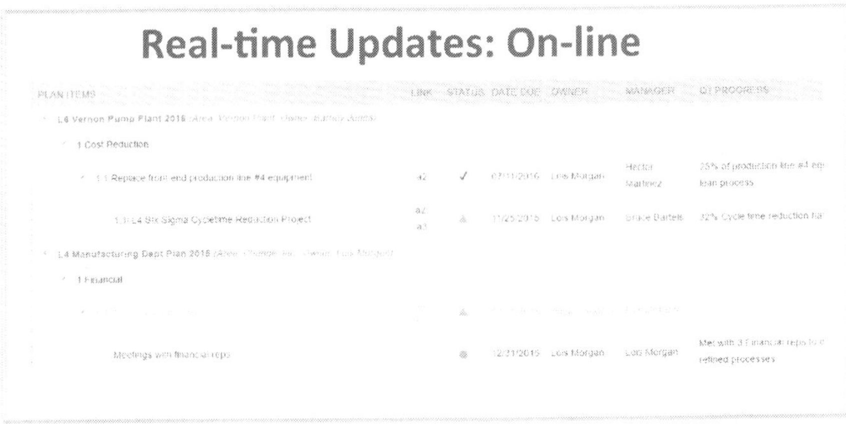

status of her committed *deliverables* along with related metrics. Next is the view Lois would have after clicking on a specific dashboard box. It takes her to the two department plans (Manufacturing and the Vernon Pump Plan) where she has actions that need updating. She can update the information as needed:

status, dates due, quarter comments, as well as upload any documents as needed. Lois can also see the upstream initiatives (and status), as well as any manager feedback on these initiatives.

The third example below shows an individual real-time update that includes scorecard metrics across the top and details as to specific objectives and tasks below.

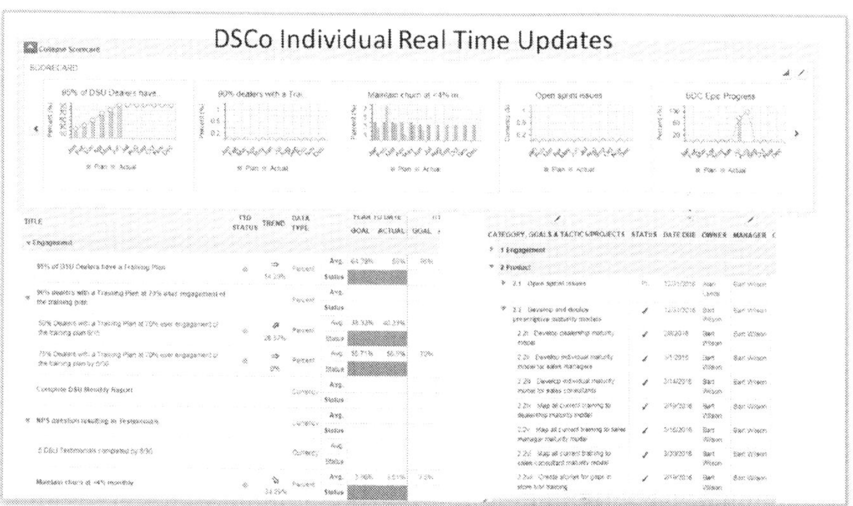

Our last example, on the next page, is of a team *real-time dashboard* that was used to track ongoing launch readiness for the high tech company's new subscription-based sales enablement business model. The leaders of each cross-functional team provided red-yellow-green variance inputs to multiple cross-functional initiatives online, which were then downloaded into a standard PowerPoint presentation for formal sharing. Online were mechanisms for leaders to share supporting information on issues driving their variance assessments, as well as links to mitigation plans as needed.

Our experience over the last decade indicates that there are five key mechanisms that must be established in order to truly drive successful real-time updating.

The first, and most important, is to establish a public and visible digital (i.e. online) location for all scorecard and dashboard information. For those unfamiliar with the terms, scorecards generally provide status information and dashboards generally provide measurement based information, such as key performance indicators (KPIs), though the two terms are often used interchangeably. There are all kinds of options to do so from smartsheet™, to collaborative applications, such as GroupMind™, to enterprise strategy management or reporting solutions, such as AgileStrategyManager® or Tableau™. In each case, the idea is to have a single online location where reporting information can be transparently made available to all who are interested in seeing it and in a form where frequent updates in real-time are possible. We acknowledge how difficult it can be to understand the value of transparency as an engagement motivator.

The same is true for portfolio, program and project information. Not only is it easier for teams to understand what's going on, but also the transparency often encourages clarity, unity and agility in major ways. For example, if project or program or portfolio objectives, strategy, benefits and measures aren't well articulated, feedback from direct and extended stakeholders, as to what additional clarity is needed, can quickly be provided. Teams can more easily rally around critical priorities when they clearly know what they are. Not only is reporting easier and more cost effective, cross-functional analysis is so much easier. Any PMO leader who has had to provide summary status across dozens of programs or projects well understands this challenge.

Thirdly, is the importance of establishing an effective metrics/KPI management process that involves agreement on the number and type of metrics/KPIs (based on the agreed upon fundamental organizing concept), their definition, owner, baseline and target metrics and variance (red-yellow-green) boundary conditions. It's also critical to establish a rigorous process for determining what to do when variance boundaries are broken. Should an action plan be created? Should a *tiger team* be created? If so, what is its mandate and when should it deliver results? Should the strategy be revisited and modified? If the goal is now unattainable how should the *higher ups* be informed?

The fourth process that needs to be structured and institutionalized is a prioritization process, which also should be as real-time as possible. All kinds of tools exist, both Excel-based and online via Likert-scale evaluations to Check Vote, (High-Medium-Low), Multi-scale and Stack Ranking processes. What is critical, though, is that whatever mechanism is put in place that it be data-driven rather than gut-feel driven. This isn't to say that gut-feel doesn't have a place, but its place should be at the decision-making level after a prioritization process has been instituted.

The last mechanism that needs to be established is the appropriate issues escalation process. For some organizations, only issues involving *Red* variances are escalated. For others, only those related to specific strategic risks are escalated. Either way, agreement needs to be made at all levels as to how, when and what issues get escalated and the related decision-making process to get them resolved, which we'll discuss in detail in the next section.

Now, as can be seen in the example below from Google, senior leadership can play a major role in driving compliance and overall performance achievement.

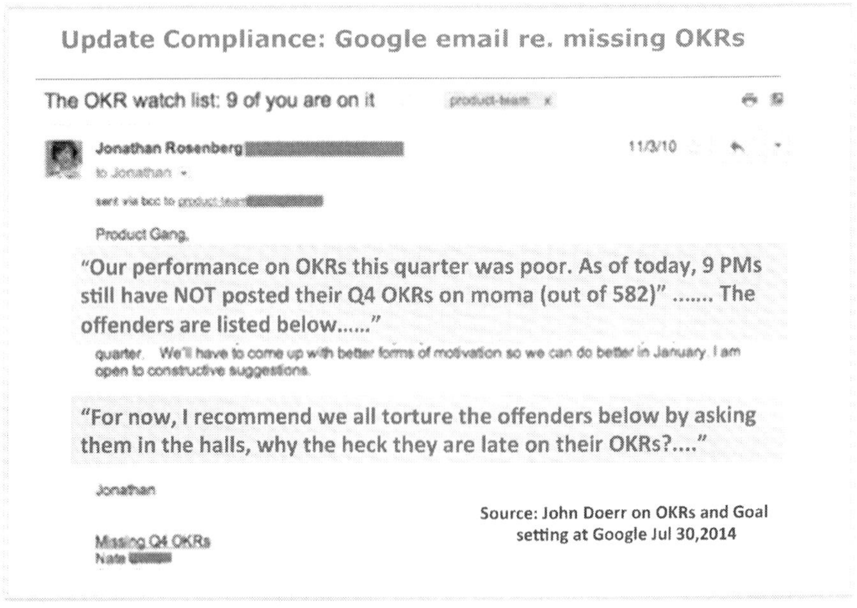

BENEFITS OF REAL-TIME UPDATES

The benefits to this type of approach are significant. Not only do they improve decision-making quality, but they also reduce decision-making cycle time. The value of real-time summary reporting is self-evident, especially when there is open and transparent access to all participants. More importantly, when online reports, scorecards and dashboards can be personalized to meet the needs of various leaders at various levels of the organization, effectively and easily, organizational agility is dramatically strengthened. At the tactical level, *doing the right things right* can be more than just a slogan, it can become a way of *being*. Note that the implementation of this type of process is not easy and requires significant change management. Core to success is an iterative process involving continuous, ongoing timely communications as well as group and individual training and coaching. For our mid-west power supplier, this involved hands-on user training, customized help guides and cheat sheets, *how to* videos, as well as standard *meeting-in-a-box*, glossary of terms, help hotlines and FAQs for every step in the process.

CADENCE DECISIONS

Cadence decision-making means the establishment of formal collaboration meetings involving linked cohorts, which could be a Run-the-Business team, strategic initiative portfolio leaders, senior leadership team members, cross-functional extended teams or whatever. The focus of such meetings is to make decisions. They are not status meetings. They are not *INFORM* meetings. They are designed to ensure proactive real-time resource reallocation or assignment, proactive assessment of course correcting solutions, to manage prioritization and issue resolution processes. Central to Cadence Decision meetings is the idea of comparing *current work* and *current backlog* and using cross-functional collaboration to reprioritize *current backlog* based on current performance realities in a flexible way. It's important to remember that *current backlog* could refer to a wide variety of work efforts including lower priority initiatives, unfunded ideas, existing program or activities enhancements to name a few. Using the enFOCUS Sprint Scrum as a model, in the Agile Strategy Execution Workflow below we have added variance analysis (comparisons of actual performance to target) that can trigger *team sprints*, and/or *self-meetings* to assess progress, which feed the *Cadence Decisions*, which in turn can feed reprioritization processes.

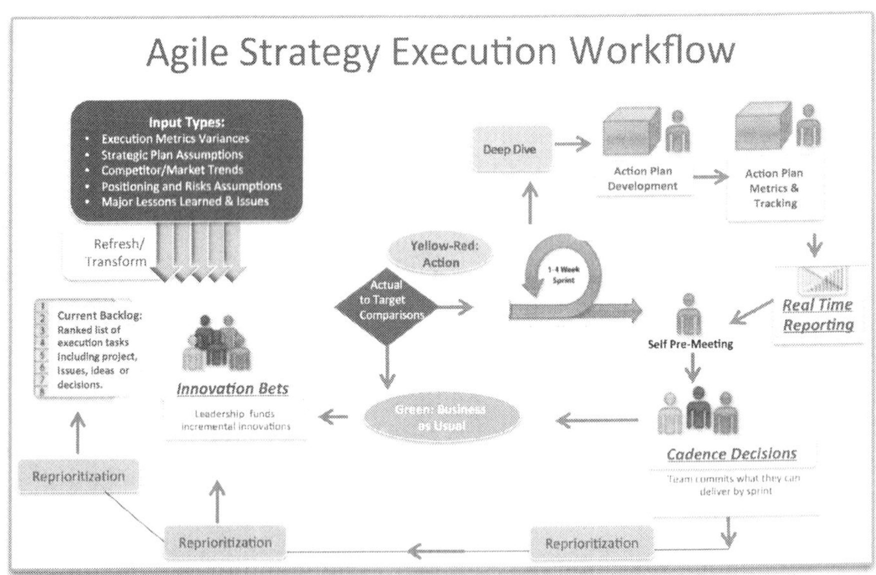

This image also shows how the *Innovation Bets* and *Refresh/Transform* dimensions fit, which will be discussed in the next sections.

The Cadence Decisions processes also enable teams to share and analyze performance, engage in self-directed *test and learn* activities, thereby better understanding their group mind. The truth is that for most teams, as GroupMind™ collaboration activities have demonstrated, their *"collective intelligence is greater than the sum of their parts."*

CADENCE DECISIONS SUCCESS EXAMPLES

The example below illustrates what happens when a Detailed Plan (as shared in Dimension #1) is updated in real-time and then the impacts are discussed at a cross-functional team *Cadence Decisions* meeting. In this scenario, Laurie is unable to meet her deliverable date so the status of her *Define Epic* turns red. The team is able to directly see that Joel's ability to meet his cost reduction goal may be severely impacted. Instead of just reporting status, the meeting focus will now be on what mitigating activities or course corrections or tactical pivots can be undertaken to reduce the impact of the missed date on the team's success in reducing both costs of all

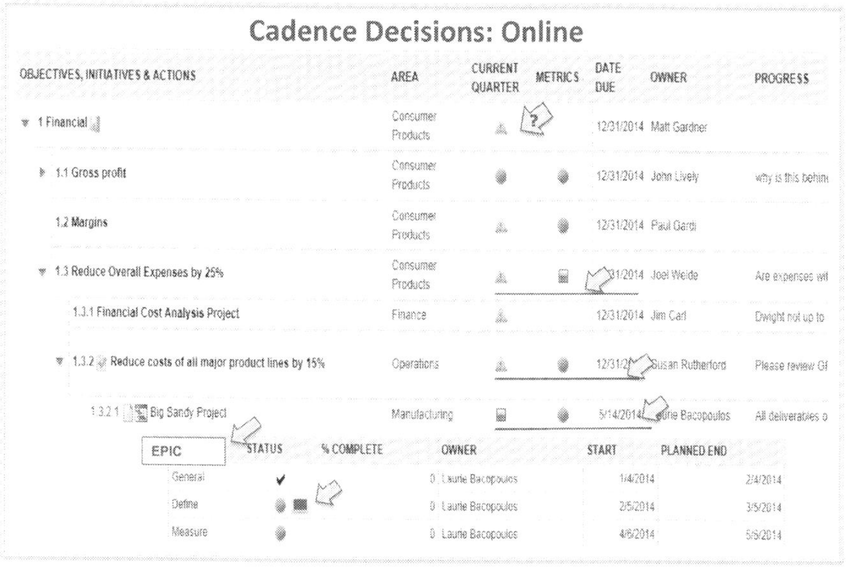

Cadence Decisions: Online

OBJECTIVES, INITIATIVES & ACTIONS	AREA	CURRENT QUARTER	METRICS	DATE DUE	OWNER	PROGRESS
1 Financial	Consumer Products			12/31/2014	Matt Gardner	
1.1 Gross profit	Consumer Products			12/31/2014	John Lively	why is this behin
1.2 Margins	Consumer Products			12/31/2014	Paul Gardi	
1.3 Reduce Overall Expenses by 25%	Consumer Products			31/2014	Joel Welde	Are expenses wi
1.3.1 Financial Cost Analysis Project	Finance			12/31/2014	Jim Carl	Dwight not up to
1.3.2 Reduce costs of all major product lines by 15%	Operations			12/31/2	Susan Rutherford	Please review Gl
1.3.2.1 Big Sandy Project	Manufacturing			5/14/2014	urie Bacopoulos	All deliverables o

EPIC	STATUS	% COMPLETE	OWNER	START	PLANNED END
General	✔	0	Laurie Bacopoulos	1/4/2014	2/4/2014
Define		0	Laurie Bacopoulos	2/5/2014	3/5/2014
Measure		0	Laurie Bacopoulos	4/6/2014	5/6/2014

major product lines by 15% and the higher level goal of reducing overall expenses by 25%. Below is an example of the cadence decision-making governance process established by Jared Hamilton, CEO at Driving Sales (DS). It illustrates an example of a typical on-line review process.

Driving Sales Cadence Decisions Meetings Structure

Monthly:

- Each GMT wins & losses captured against their monthly ops. goals & displayed on their whiteboard
- Public whiteboards are to encourage open collaboration between depts. to achieve operational goals.
- All numbers & initiative's progress summarized & updated monthly into ASM (Agile Strategy Manager).

Bi Weekly Meeting (Interdepartmental General Strategy)

- All managers meeting to discuss inter-departmental dependencies, strategy & financial performance
- Prior to meeting, managers are to update their departmental progress against their operational goals.
- It is important that all mgmt. attends the meetings, having read the emails from each department, reviewed the #'s in ASM and worksheets/Jira, prepared to discuss issues & potential solutions to these issues, interdepartmentally.

These meetings are <u>not for updates</u>; updates are expected to happen before the meeting, but are for:

- Deciding on collaborative actions for a. identifying opportunities & b. removing roadblocks.
- Presenting new DS direction & solicit feedback (as necessary).
- Re-prioritizing backlog items & resources as necessary.

ASM is used as the real-time operating meeting agenda for the management meetings

- Updates to the items due dates, priority & comments can be updated in ASM or written in other locations, with hyperlinks accessible to all from ASM.

Cadence Decisions begin with individual updates and assessments that drive individual performance analysis and course corrections of those activities that are under the control of the individual. Depending upon the severity of the course correction, this could lead to a domino effect for all aligned and linked work. Aligned and linked team progress reviews, based on analysis of variances or of problem areas, can lead to the creation of solid action plans with specific due dates, owners and identification of needed support resources, collective buy-in on the course corrections needed or proactive *Stop-Start-Continue* decision-making. It can lead to innovative problem solving. As indicated previously, these are not *INFORM* meetings. Expectations must be set that all members will review updates before the meeting, and will be uninvited to participate in the decision-making process, if they can't do so. Cadence Decisions tend to be generally tactical in nature and manage prioritization and backlog of tasks and activities, whereas *Innovation Bets* tend to focus on adjustments to strategy.

BENEFITS OF CADENCE DECISIONS

The most important benefit of enabling cadence decision-making processes is that initiatives and tactics can be refined and pivoted in real-time so staying on track becomes much simpler. In addition, as illustrated on the previous page, it is easier to see the implications of missing targets and respond accordingly. They also enable the organizational integration of processes to identify and prioritize backlog, based on the level and type of resources and funding available. Lastly, such processes strengthen organizational agility and responsiveness.

INNOVATION BETS

Clayton Christianson, Harvard's Kim B. Clark Professor of Business Administration and the leading authority on disruptive innovation, suggests that the reason firms need to write down their strategy is so that *"they can find out what else to do that might more effectively enable the attainment of team goals."* Studies have shown that 85% of start-ups end up at IPO (Initial Public Offering) having completely pivoted from what they started out thinking their value proposition and strategy were going to be. The process that is typically used to enable this pivoting usually involves putting a stake in the ground, trying to go in that direction and if the strategy isn't working, to quickly change and try something new. In other words, teams are making incremental *Innovation Bets* that involve periodic assessments and adjusting strategy, backlog and operating priorities predominately based on incremental shifts in performance trends, risks or ongoing difficulty in resolving issues and roadblocks that arise.

Innovation Bets focus on enabling an opportunity to reflect on *emerging strategies* appearing on the horizon and initiate small actions to study, pilot or test a new or different approach. These could come from evolving or emerging trends that are becoming evident from shifts in customers, competitor or market perspectives. The goal is to use formal brainstorming techniques to ascertain whether or not an investment should be made in studying, piloting, or testing some sort of refinement, shift, pivot or other type of innovation in response to any of these *emerging strategies*. In an extreme case, the entire strategic investment portfolio could be reprioritized and other initiatives or work efforts in *current backlog* brought to the forefront.

Another interesting approach comes from Jim Bandrowski, President of Rock Your Industry, a consulting and training firm specializing in strategic innovation, process breakthrough and execution excellence. Bandrowski has developed a new process called *Wave Thinking,* which *"amplifies conventional innovation approaches by having individuals and teams ride a mental sine wave."* By engaging in what he calls a *Breakthrough Sprint,* participants:

- Think in constructively negative ways to discover unmet and unknown needs both in the industry and the organization (what he calls *Breakthrough Opportunity Areas).*
- Think in passionately positive ways to define ideal solutions to the needs (what he calls *Creative Leaps).*
- Open-mindedly bring wild ideas down to earth to form potentially feasible *Breakthrough Concepts.*
- Assess and prioritize each concept's innovation potential

using four key criteria, namely attractiveness, feasibility, synergy and timing.

- Iteratively prototype, user test, and collect feedback to refine them and select the best one.
- Develop a flexible Strategic Action Plan for execution excellence.

Below is an example of a *Breakthrough Sprint* for the hypothetical steps taken to develop a new wine industry product, from his soon to be published book on the topic of leading strategic innovation.

Wave Thinking℠ – Powering a Breakthrough Sprint℠

(Source: Forthcoming book titled *Rock Your Industry* by Jim Bandrowski, *RockYourIndustry.com*)

Breakthrough Wave℠ (Summary)			Innovation Potential*				Strategic Action Plan	
Breakthrough Opportunity Areas℠ (Unmet or Unknown Needs)	**Creative Leaps** (Wild Ideas)	**Breakthrough Concepts** (Potentially Feasible Solutions)	Attract-iveness (H,M,L) H = High	Feasi-bility (H,M,L) M = Medium	Synergy (H,M,L) L = Low	Timing (S,M,L) Short, Medium, or Long	**User Test Feedback** (Iterations of Prototypes, User Tests, and Feedback)	***Execution Excellence℠* Plan**
Wine bottles are difficult to open with regular corkscrews, dual-prong cork removers, or even elegant lever devices.	Fantasy wine opener is simply held over a bottle and the cork magically removes itself.	Motor operated. Automatically senses the cork and starts. Rechargeable battery. Operated by120-volt wire and plug for more power.	H H H M-L	H M H H	H H H L	M M S S	Reduce size and weight of cylindrical device. Have it eject the cork at the end of the cycle. Have an unjamming button.	Design: metal spiral is recessed so the corkscrew locks on the bottle and the cork is pulled straight out. Add foil cutter top. Introduce product to the market.
Same	Same	Vacuum device sucks cork out of bottle.	M-L	L	M	L	Device sucked wine out too.	Put in Innovation Vault (for later)

*Definitions: Attractiveness—To market and company. Feasibility—Will it work? Synergy—Aligns with our other strategies. Timing—Short, Medium, or Long term until revenue.

On the following pages are some other tools that can be used to drive the assessment of possible Innovation Bets. These include Quality Function Deployment (QFD) *market watch* opportunities or opportunity plans, Systems Thinking's Opportunity Planning Matrix, and SKEPTIC for future external environmental scanning. SKEPTIC helps the team identify potential future opportunities and threats that might impact the plan's execution.

Quality Function Deployment (QFD)

INTERACTIONS:
- xx Strong negative relationship
- x Mild negative relationship
- ⊛ Mild positive relationship
- O Strong positive realtionship

RELATIONSHIPS:
- ⊛ Strong relationship
- o Moderate relationship
- Δ Weak relationship

Customer Reqmts \ Product Design Reqmts	Priority	Bleed air ducting to interface Pt. A	Low APU weight	Low turbine wheel weight	High equivalent shaft horse power	Controlled turbine inlet temperature	Turbine assy. tri-hub containment	Strong internal containment ring	Lightweight containment ring	Competitive Evaluations (1–5)
Cust. envelope/interface	3	⊛						⊛		x o
Max.Weight 160lbs.	4	O	⊛	O			O		⊛	o x
Bleed air 75 lbs/min	4	O			⊛	⊛				o x
Turbine containment	5			O		O	⊛	⊛		ox
Elect pwr. 40KVA	3				⊛					x o
Reliable	5			O		⊛				xo
Support oil-cooled gen.	5		O							o x
* * *										
Technical Evaluations (5–1)		x o	x o	x o	x o	o x	o x	x o	x o	
Target Value		Target Loc.	168lb	<8 lb	350hp	1850°	2.5 lb @Pwr	3 lb @Pwr	<8 lb	
Technical Difficulty		1	4	3	5	3	4	2	4	
Importance Rating		39	35	42	35	60	52	40	20	

Evaluations:
- x We
- o XYZ Co.

SKEPTIC Future EXTERNAL Environmental Scanning / Trends

List the 5-10 environmental trends - projections - opportunities - threats facing us over the life of our plan:

S Socio-Demographics (People / Society):

K Competition / Substitutes:

E Economics:

E Ecology (Including Natural Disasters):

P Political / Regulatory:

T Technical:

I Industry / Suppliers:

C Customer / Citizens:

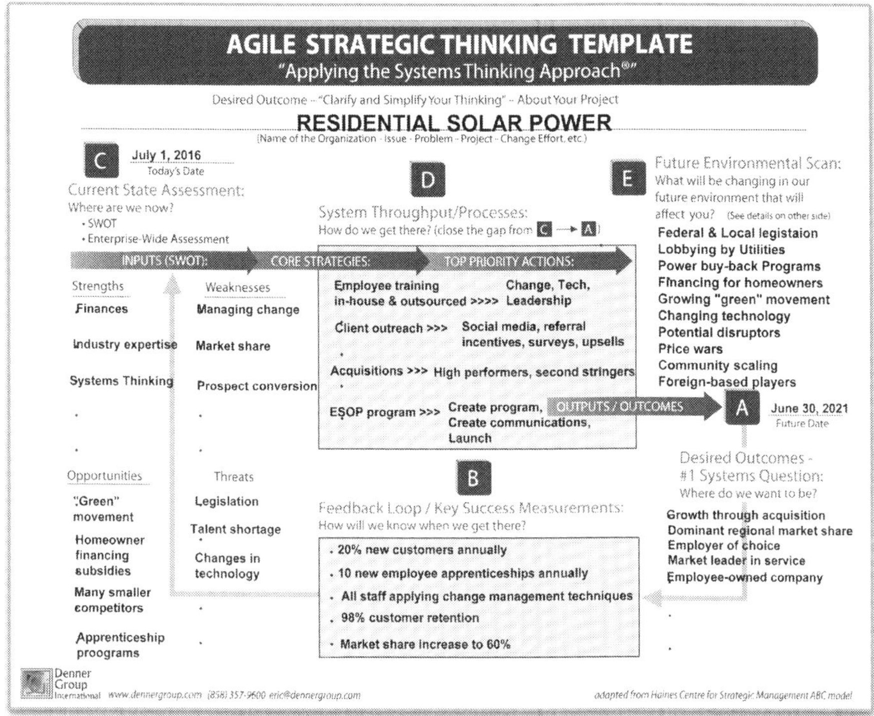

INNOVATION BETS SUCCESS EXAMPLES

An example of a very successful innovation bet took place at the large high tech company. The then head of Services Sales, realized that a number of customers were moving away from *purchasing* and were starting to get interested in *subscription-based* models. In discussing this new trend at a strategic initiative portfolio quarterly update meeting, a decision was made to fund a three-month effort by a cross-functional team to assess the implications of this new selling model and develop recommendations. Based on that work, a new customer success organization was designed and was operational within 16 months, which was a dramatic pivot for the company.

Below is an example of an Innovation Bets process and meeting agenda at DSCo, our start-up in the automobile industry. By instituting this process, the firm realized through one Innovation Bet that customers really liked the idea of a centralized portal or platform from which to get access to all of their services, which has led to a major pivot for the entire firm towards building this capability.

DSCo Quarterly Innovation Bets Governance: Example

Quarterly Innovation Bets mgmt. meetings are action meetings, conducted to:

- Briefly review briefly goals and progress
- Discuss "Market Watch" opportunities/emerging trends in the market
- Recommend small/big bets (deep dives) needed to address potential gaps/opportunities
- Prioritize & decide on additional studies/small/big bets we should take on next quarter
- Re-align resources to high priority initiatives

Results of the meeting are:

- Prioritization of new opportunities
- Pivoting/putting on hold current activities that are lower in the priority list
- Development of timeframes to address these issues and seize on opportunities.

Next steps include:

- Discuss opportunities with our Core leaders to determine scope and resources
- Flush out action plans
- Enter action plans into ASM (Agile Strategy Manager)™

BENEFITS OF INNOVATION BETS

The key benefit of the Innovation Bets dimension is that it formalizes an organization's focus on ongoing innovation, and enables a process and environment for agile experimentation. Of course, it assumes that some sort of funding pool and tracking process exists so that the effectiveness of each dollar spent can be assessed.

REFRESH OR TRANSFORM

The Refresh or Transform dimension involves the periodic formal reassessment of the ongoing *deliberate* strategy including any needed revisions to core business assumptions and any required renewing, updating or revising of strategic or operating plans, priorities, linkages or alignment. Ideally, this process should take place before budget cycles are underway. They should include a wide variety of both outside-in and inside-out assessments. These could include technical, sociological, economic and political environmental scans at a country level or perhaps even on a global basis. They could deep dive updates to the original market and competitive analyses or new benchmarking studies.

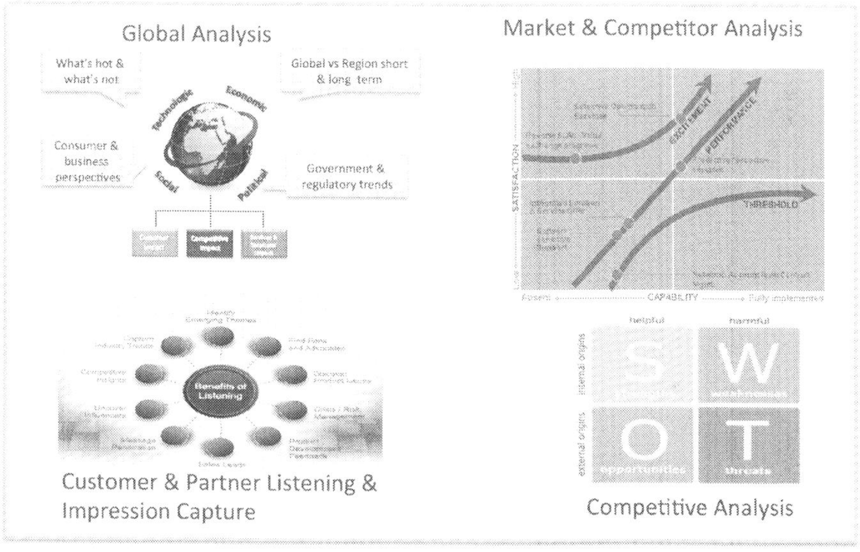

Reassessment of customer and partner listening program results all helps to improve decision-making cycle time, thereby reducing the potential for *not-in-my-backyard* syndrome and improving Time-to-Value and strategic investment Return on Investment (ROI).

All kinds of tools exist for these types of analytical assessments, including the SKEPTIC tool mentioned in the section discussing the Detail Plans and Metrics dimension, SWOT Analysis (Strengths, Weaknesses, Opportunities and Threats) and Kano Analysis (categorizing features and benefits that enable customer delight or dissatisfaction).

These kinds of meetings can also be used to assess whether or not the team or organization has the right business or operating model in place or whether or not it is delivering the results expected when they are expected. It can also be used to drive assessments of budgets or rolling quarter financial variances or assess whether or not there are new skills needed or strengths that need to be developed. Most organizations have in place, ongoing strategic planning processes that work generally pretty well. For many, these are tied into budget planning cycles. Below is a simple graphic illustrating a typical Refresh or Transform meeting planning process. They generally have three components. The first component is a situation analysis whose objective is to collect relevant opinions from as many perspectives as possible, ask questions and uncover facts. The second phase is to assess options by asking a wide variety of brainstorming questions and exercises to develop insights and generate alternatives. Last is to make decisions, and from there define the roadmap for the future, which promotes effective action.

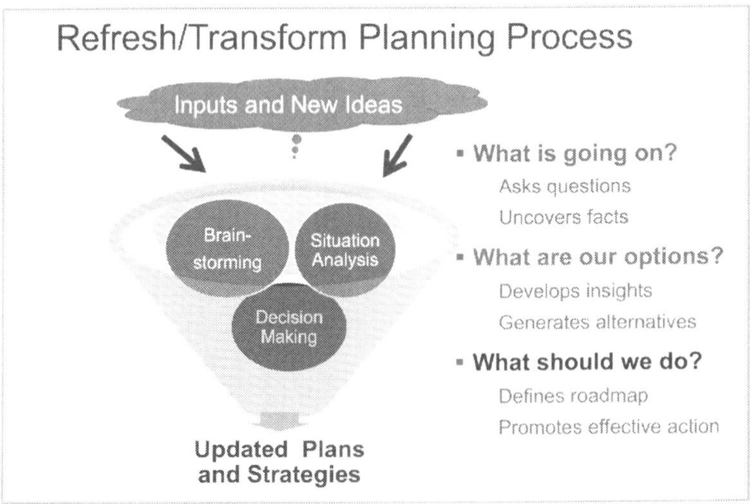

In the Appendix is an example of a detailed planning workflow that can be used to facilitate all kinds of Refresh or Transform discussions. The big change is that no longer can these processes take place on an annual basis. As Jeff Immelt, CEO of General Electric has shared:

"We've basically unplugged anything that was annual. In the digital age, sitting down once a year to do anything is weird, it's just bizarre. So whether it's doing business reviews or strategic planning, it's in a much more continuous way."

BENEFITS OF REFRESH AND TRANSFORM

The most important benefit of this dimension is improved decision-making cycle time and agility. By enabling the review and reassessment of value propositions for key priorities based on updated trends and *market watch* data, the firm is able to make timely course corrections when needed. They also help to quickly ascertain if the Innovation Bets are generating the results desired.

DIMENSIONS SUMMARY

Often a question that comes up from time to time is to ask about the suggested frequency of the various formal and informal meetings required to drive effective Dimension accountability and responsiveness. There are no hard and fast rules, other than the fact that the old approaches of yearly planning and high-level quarterly strategic initiative readouts no longer are relevant. With the help of Laurie Bacopoulos from Cobblestone Consulting, on the next page we've created an ASE Framework™ meeting cadence summary and applied it to the Driving Sales environment. Baselines are established on a yearly basis for *Plans & Metrics* and *Align and Link,* which are then refined, at least quarterly, based on Cadence

Decision results. *Real-Time Updates* includes daily, weekly, monthly and quarterly activities. *Cadence Decisions* activities will vary depending upon the size of the organization, but at the leadership level, they should occur at least quarterly. Area or department level discussions should occur monthly or bi-weekly and of course at the team level should occur at least weekly. The same is true of *Innovation Bets*. At a minimum they should be quarterly, though this will vary directly on the firms' funding strategy. The general view according to Gary Hamel, in his book The Future of Management, is that there should be multiple sources of experimental capital and that *"efforts must be made to make it easy for funding sources and new ideas to find each other."*

Driving Sales ASE Framework™ Meeting Cadence

Dimension	Purpose	Yearly	Quarterly	Monthly	Weekly	Daily	Responsible
Plans & Metrics	Translate objectives into area plans & metrics	Baseline established	Refine based on cadence decisions				Execs & Area/Dept. Mgrs.
Align & Link	Align and link goals, strategies & operating plans	Baseline established	Refinement based on cadence decisions				Execs & Area/ Dept. Mgrs.
Real-Time Updates	Drive real-time plan updates based on day-to-day triggers for prioritized backlog		ASM updates on objectives, initiatives, portfolios & epics	ASM updates on epics/ initiatives	Jira update: sprint stories/ epics	Story/task update on dept. boards	Area/Dept. Leads & Work Teams
Cadence Decisions	Ensure appropriate resourcing & course correcting solutions to manage and prioritize backlog		Refine backlog and schedule based on initiative progress				Mgmt. Team
				Bi-Wkly. backlog adjustments			Area/Dept. Mgrs.
					Sprint meetings	Informal discussions	Dept. sprint teams
Innovation Bets	Identify and assess opportunities for innovation		Formal decisions on priority & go forward actions	Exploration & discussion of market trends	Internal sensing of market		Execs, Area/ Dept. Leads & Staff
Refresh/ Transform	Identify and assess opportunities for innovation	Finalize plan	Pivots/refinements as necessary				Execs & Dept. Leads

Now that we've explained the various dimensions of our Agile Strategy Execution™, let's take a look at the Influencing Factors that can make or break any attempts at enabling more agile strategy execution.

INFLUENCING FACTORS

IMPACTS OF CULTURE

As summarized below from a variety of sources on the topic, every organization has a culture with a set of formal and informal attributes, which usually include some or all of the following:

- ***Archetypes*** - is the organization military-like, family-like, church-like or government-like?
- ***Leadership Focus*** - How do the leaders actually lead? Is leadership based on participative team building and coaching? Is it authoritative, commanding, directing and tough-minded? Is it visionary and based on pushing the limits and a safe place for experimentation? Is it empowering and inspiring?
- ***Ways to Success*** - How does the company succeed? Is it through synergy and teamwork? Is it by controlling information? Is it by being the *best*? Is it through domination? Is it by focusing on strengths?

- ***Power Focus*** - Where is real power focused? Is it based on formal roles and positions or is it built on relationships? Does expertise win the day or is it charisma?
- ***Employee Role*** - How are employees supposed to work? Are they to follow directives and adhere to specific role expectations? Are they to be team players and contribute to the broader whole effort and take the initiative in areas outside their direct ownership? Are they expected to develop narrow or broad areas of expertise and competence? Are they to be versatile and open to growth and change?
- ***Key Norms*** - What are the key norms that operate? Is the environment driving towards order, standardization and discipline or is it based on competition and only the strong survive? Is it a meritocracy with craftsmanship valued? Is there freedom to make mistakes and learn from them? Are dedication and commitment rewarded?
- ***Change*** - What is the organization's philosophy about change? Is it resistant or open? Is change embraced or does it have to be proactively driven or mandated?
- ***Decisions*** - How are key decisions made? Is the environment participative and consensus-oriented or is it analytical, rational and data driven? Is the process methodical and formula oriented or is it highly participative, dynamic and informal?
- ***Climate*** - What is the day-to-day climate really like? Is everyone serious and formal, intense and fast paced? Is it generous, compassionate, and relaxed or is it of the work hard/play hard variety?

- ***Customer Experience*** - And finally, what about the organization's attitude towards customers? Are relationships with customers partnerships or do they come because of the firm's *one-of-a-kind* offerings or *state-of-the-art* solutions or is it the only game in town?

According to leading experts in the field, culture matters because it:

- Provides consistency for an organization and its people.
- Provides order and structure.
- Establishes an internal *way of life* for people (boundaries, ground rules, formal/informal communication patterns, membership criteria).
- Determines conditions for internal effectiveness (rewards, punishment, expectations, priorities, nature and use of power).
- Sets patterns for internal relationships amongst people.
- Defines effective and ineffective performance.
- Frames and is framed by company values.

However, as has been attributed to Peter Drucker, *Culture Eats Strategy for Breakfast,* which is another way of saying that if the core culture is resistant to improving agile strategy execution, it will be an uphill battle without senior management support and sponsorship and the use of proactive culture change mechanisms. In fact, it may be an uphill battle even with all of those levels of support, as existing corporate cultures and value systems can be enabling or disabling drivers. Another influencing factor can be the level of employee engagement. As mentioned previously, recent Gallup surveys indicate that on average worldwide, only about 13% of employees are engaged at work, leaving 65% not engaged, and another 25% actively disengaged. Now some of this can be attributed to the growth in the contingent workers either due to the outsourcing of functions or due to staff augmentation workforce talent management strategies. Note also that culture change can be perceived as seriously destabilizing, especially if there is any hint that the change might violate a specific set of values or beliefs or if it generates any sort of embarrassment or fear of failure. In addition, resistance will increase if the change involves unmet expectations or thwarted intentions or if it runs counter to any individual or group view of what needs to or should happen. In

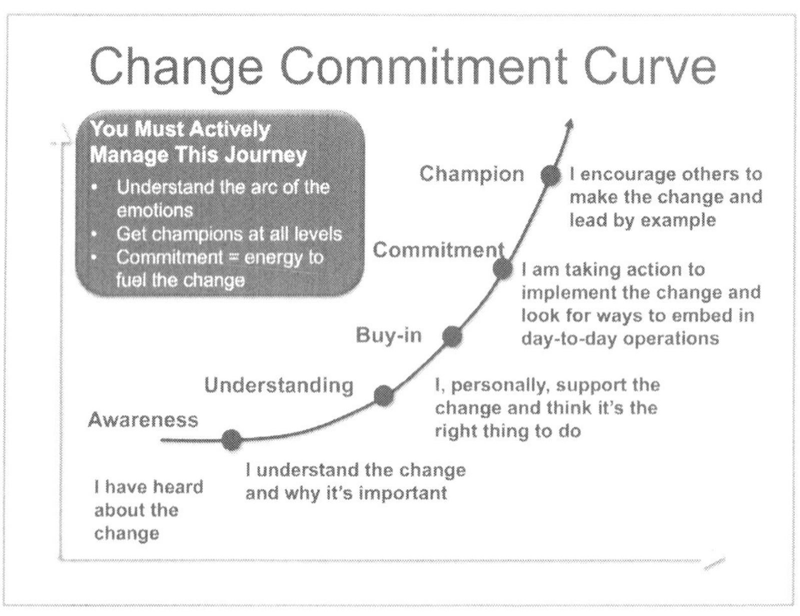

an ideal world, organizations always hope that change occurs in an upward arcing pattern, as illustrated in the above figure. Alas, the reality is that change more frequently happens like this figure on the next page. Change adoption begins with denial and then progresses through the *Valley of Despair* to eventual acceptance, hope, energy and enthusiasm. As Ed Catmull, Co-founder & President, Pixar Animation described in his 2014 book Creativity, Inc., *"Fear of change (that is innate, stubborn and resistant to reason) – is a powerful force. We cling as long as possible to the perceived safe place that we already know, refusing to loosen our grip, until we feel sure another safe place awaits us."*

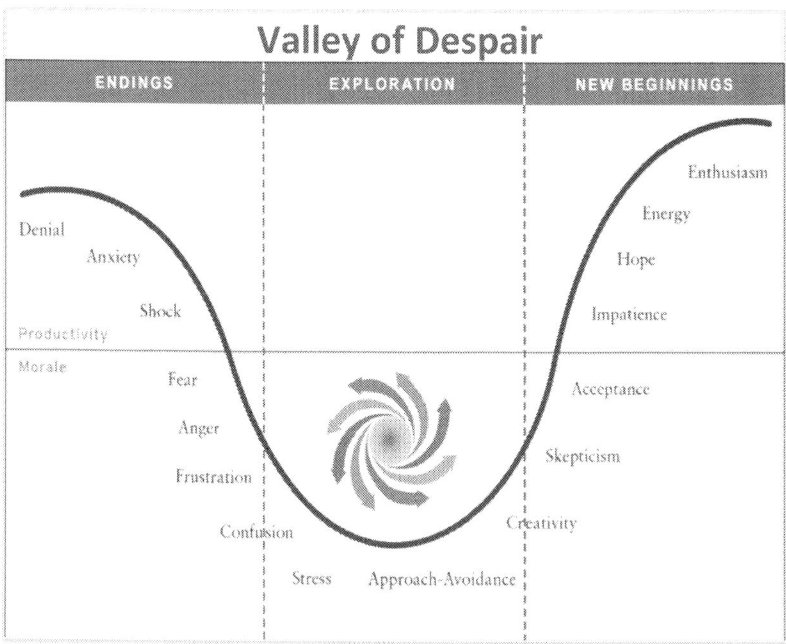

In addition, there are significant barriers to learning and adapting to change as described by Jim Ewing in his Change Loop Model outlined on the next page. Needless to say, new knowledge or ways of doing things doesn't come easily and often-insufficient attention is paid to address these issues. A number of methods exist, mostly from the change management field that can be adopted including:

- Culture and Climate Mapping
- Stakeholder Impact Assessment and Engagement Enablement
- Change Branding and Storytelling

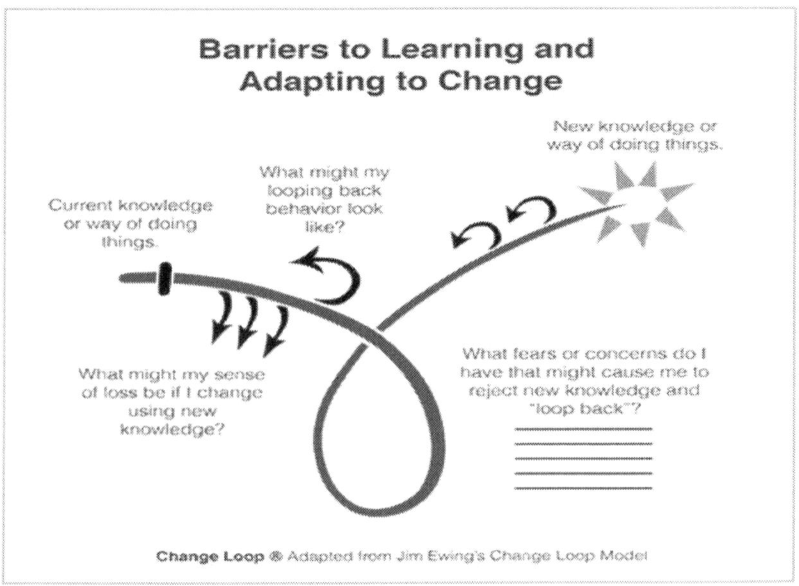

CULTURE AND CLIMATE MAPPING

Most organizations also have a set of preached vs. practiced cultural dynamics. The classic example is the implementation of management *'open-door'* policies. Most organizations today preach the accessibility of managers and the idea that at any time employees are welcome to *walk in the door* and share their concerns or brainstorm new ideas without penalty. However, more often than not, the reality is that getting on the manager's calendar is difficult. When an appointment is made, managers are often distracted (especially if the meeting is via teleconference and not in person) or not skilled in active listening, resulting in unsatisfactory employee engagement. In other words, the door may be open, but if employees don't want to cross the threshold, then the practiced cultural intent is very different from that preached.

William Schneider, in his 1994 book The Reengineering Alternative – A Plan for Making Your Current Culture Work, suggests that every firm has a dominant culture and that there are generally only four kinds. Some firms are control-oriented and care about order and security whereas others focus on collaboration and affiliation as the key value. In some environments competence and achievement trump all, whereas for other environments the focus might be on experience cultivation and self-actualization. Survey instruments

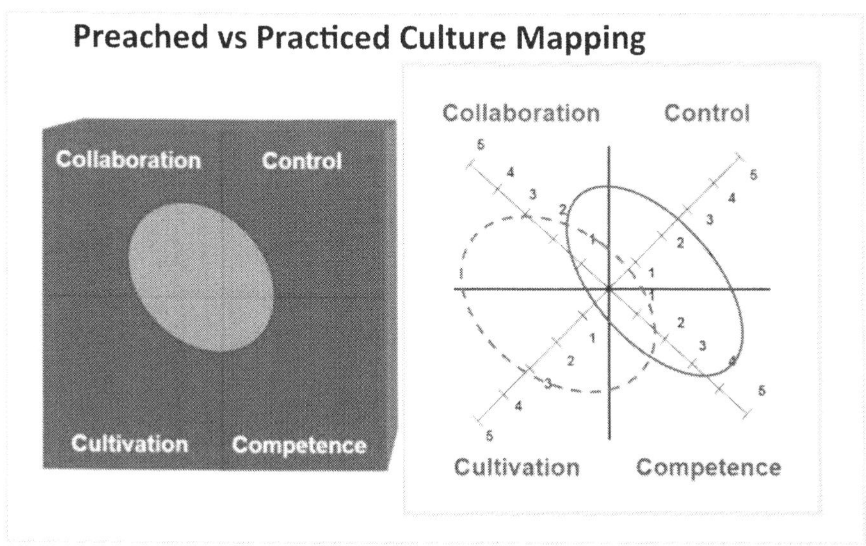

can be used to assess and establish a baseline understanding of a firm's existing core culture.

Once there is awareness of the core culture, leaders can then assess the size of any various gaps between where the organization aspires to be and where it is today. Then plans can be put in place to enable whatever shifts are needed so that there is greater synergy between what is preached and what is practiced. In addition, if significant culture change is required, the extent of the task can be identified. In our experience so far, one of the largest culture shifts often required involves helping the leadership team embrace business digitization.

STAKEHOLDER IMPACT ASSESSMENT AND EMPLOYEE ENGAGEMENT ENABLEMENT

Once the type and magnitude of the desired culture changes have been identified, specific stakeholders, be they individuals, groups or cohorts, need to be identified and the relative impact of the desired change on them assessed. By understanding both the change type (organizational, operational or cultural) and the degree of impact, (H, M, L) strategy execution practitioners can determine how best to engage with that particular team, cohort or individual. It's important to acknowledge that culture change adoption doesn't really occur like a waterfall, or a loop or a valley or an upward evolving curve. Change occurs more like what happens when a pebble is dropped into a still pond. Like the illustration below, each expanding concentric circle represents larger and larger groups or cohorts that get engaged with the change over time. It is only over

- **Trendsetters** - Message Leaders: Core Team
- **Evangelists** - Message Champions: Cross-Functional Message Ambassadors
- **Advocates** - Message Committed: Connected Cohorts
- **Change Stakeholders** - Messages for Understanding
- **Change Influencers** - Messages for Awareness

Each circle has different engagement methods and it could require up to a dozen 'touch points' to engage. Industry best practice is 7-14 'interactions' for full engagement.

time that the *Tipping Point* is reached that enables the transition to proactive, collective change adoption. Two innovative digital employee engagement strategies, which have generated good success, are based on the use of real-time web-enabled collaboration platforms. These include *Impression Capture™* and *Crowd Accelerated Individualized Learning™* (CAIL™).

IMPRESSION CAPTURE™

Though survey mechanisms have been used forever as a way to understand how individuals, teams and cohorts view a particular topic or concern, there are some serious limitations with them. Not only are response rates usually poor, but also with few direct or timely feedback mechanisms, participants often feel like their feedback ends up in a *deep black hole*. A new engagement mechanism, called *Impression Capture™,* that is starting to gain traction, is the idea of using real-time collaboration software to enable instant feedback, not just to the survey creators but also at the same time to the participants.

As illustrated below, engagement happens through the use of audio, video, image and text modalities to introduce the topic at hand. The survey mechanism is enabled in such a way that teams or

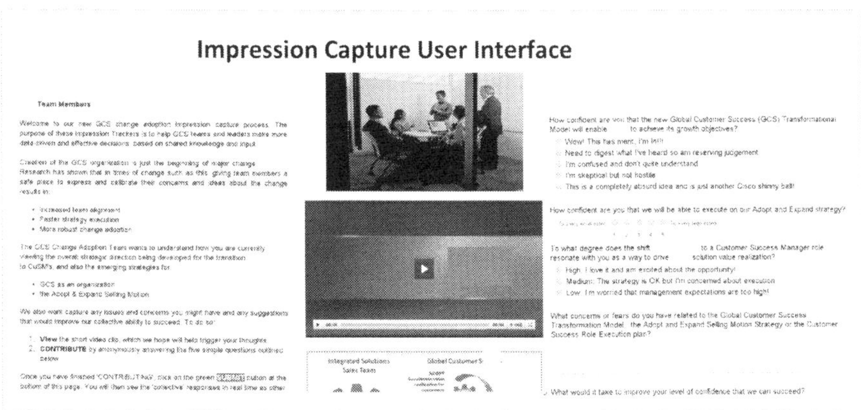

cohorts can access the platform in the moment and see how everyone else in the cohort has responded. It's amazing what a difference such a small change can make in response rates. An *Impression Capture™* process was initiated by our large high tech company to assess one of the cohort team's views of a specific strategy and individual role change. The response rate was an amazingly high 65%. Participants provided detailed qualitative inputs, outlining not just their perceived issues and concerns but also specific and actionable direction to management on how these issues could effectively be resolved.

CROWD ACCELERATED INDIVIDUALIZED LEARNING™

Another new change adoption engagement construct originated from work done by GroupMind Express, a leader in web-enabled collaboration, with the Stanford University Graduate School of Business' Center for Leadership. Using multi-media engagement mechanisms such as video, audio, image, text and Socratic questioning modalities, participants are offered a safe environment to share perspectives, brainstorm ideas, enable participative reflection and provide constructive feedback. Change communications environments can be created that can be self-directed or facilitated by a team leader or other subject matter expert and even enable team *best idea voting*. Results, so far, are showing dramatic improvement in change adoption rates. Specifically:

- Participants are much more engaged with more in-depth sharing of change impact perspectives and constructive feedback.
- Thinking and conversation are at a much deeper level about the issues or topics being raised.
- Comments are much more in-depth and of much higher quality and more creative than traditional feedback mechanisms.
- Learning is more impactful and stickier and the building of

personal action plans reinforces personal commitment levels.

- Participants are empowered to focus more of their efforts toward shared purpose and goals.

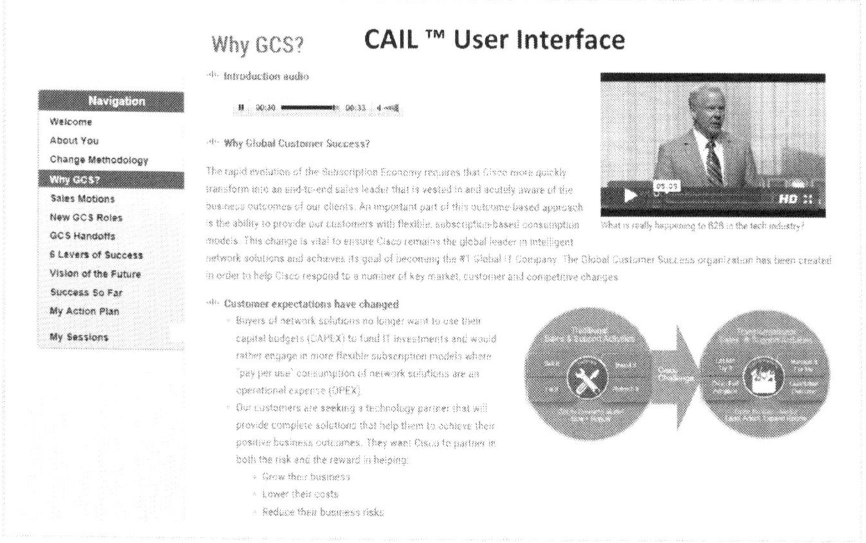

The above prototype provides an example of a typical CAIL™ user interface. There are seven topics that address:

- Why the change? (market/competitive landscape shifts).
- What is the change exactly? (new sales motions).
- Are there new roles? If so what are they and why? (Customer Success Managers and Services Renewals Specialists).
- What do the resulting handoffs to the sales organization will look like?
- How will success be measured?
- What is the leadership team's vision for the future?
- What have been the successes and track record so far?

There is also a space for participants to document their own individual change *action plans*.

Another example involves one of Silicon Valley's leading telecommunications firms that wanted to move away from their *control-oriented* culture to one that was more commitment-based. By introducing the change using a facilitated CAIL™-type employee-enablement approach, their post-session scores soared to well above 4 on a 5-point scale. Not only did participants understand the intent of the change and how trust is built or eroded in a work environment, but also they were willing to assertively work towards building a *Commitment Culture* by agreeing to personally take at least one new action to build trust within the next 30 days.

The same happened at a provider of manufacturing CAD-CAM software that initiated efforts to improve employees' understanding and usage of a newly introduced decision-making model. Belief as to whether or not the senior leadership team was making good decisions for the business improved by over 10 points, as did the employee belief that the organization had in place an effective decision-making process.

CHANGE BRANDING AND STORYTELLING

Another critical activity is the art and science of change branding, which involves the design and building of an effective change story that can be branded, marketed and communicated.

According to research done by John Kotter, at best, leaders can expect that introducing any sort of change will at first have the following impacts:

- About 30% of any typical group will believe after discussion that whatever the new thing is has merit.

- Another 30% will need to digest what they heard and another 20% will be confused.
- 10% will think the new idea is stupid and completely absurd and another 20% will be skeptical but not outright hostile.

This means that good change stories must be very clear about:

- What is the primary message about what needs to be communicated? i.e. *need to know* vs. *nice to know*.
- Who must be targeted and when? And why is it relevant to them?
- What media will be used for the interaction? What is the best vehicle for informing and engaging?
- What are the potential noise and/or barriers that might prevent the message from being absorbed?
- How do we ensure clarity and commitment? - as too much information can be worse than none.

All of us have individual concerns, purposes and circumstances. It's how people think and operate! All of us will make unsupervised decisions when clarity no longer exists or is not available. People need control! All of us are connected in different ways to other people within and outside of the organization. People talk and are influenced by many variables. There are an infinite number of external and internal influence factors that shape one's perception of an organization. It is critical that we are consistent and clear when communicating to people to ensure credibility and trust! However, the net-net is that none of this can be accomplished without a consistent *change story.* More importantly, to make a message truly stick it needs to be delivered seven times using seven different channels.

Effective change stories can help reduce the expected *Performance Dip,* accelerate culture and language change, and improve the level and type of collaboration levels and engagement. But to do so requires commitment to lots of feedback mechanisms in order to evaluate the change story effectiveness and strategy and evolve it if needed. To paraphrase John Kotter, culture change branding must:

- Cultivate a sense of urgency.
- Clearly articulate the idealized future state.
- Be designed for understanding and buy-in.
- Clearly answer the WIFM question *What's In It For Me!*
- Empower others to act.
- Produce short-term wins.
- Keep going until the new culture is created.

In summary, an organization's culture can be an enabling or disabling driver. In order for it to be truly enabling, stakeholders must be properly segmented, and proactively engaged with communication strategies and methods appropriate to stakeholder unique needs and the type of change being adopted (i.e. organizational vs. operational vs. culture). However, at the end of the day, the power of storytelling and the quality of the change story can make all the difference between creating champion change adoption and just minimal awareness or between wild success and dismal failure.

It continues to amaze us how few leadership teams make a regular practice of communicating to their teams, in a transparent way, what decisions have been made and the thinking behind them. It continues to amaze us how few leadership teams articulate well and track issues, action items and results. It continues to amaze us how few firms communicate and make widely available their strategic plan and its assumptions. It continues to amaze us how few firms translate that plan into understandable and specific goals, execution plans and related investment programs that are in turn aligned and linked throughout the organization. It continues to amaze us how many managers still manage by *Extrapolation*, *Hockey Stick*, *Crisis* and *Hope* as illustrated on the next page.

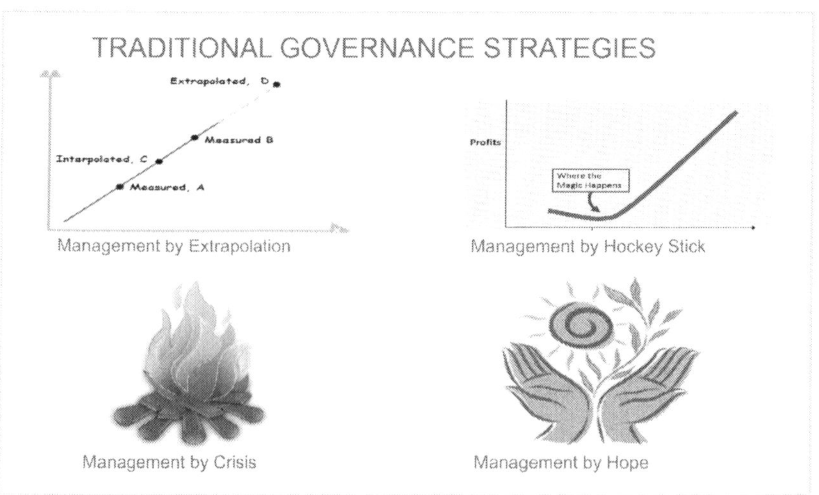

Unfortunately, moving up the **Agile Strategy Execution** maturity curve is not possible without effective real-time digital governance and decision-making processes. Whether it's called *Business Digitization* or *Connected Enablement* or *BYOD (Bring-Your-Own-Device)* or an *Anywhere-Anytime* working environment, the basic concept that we are calling Connected Governance™ involves the strengthening agility, and by definition accountability and responsiveness, by connecting leadership practices, employee engagement mechanisms and collaboration processes through a Digital Experience. Connected Governance™ requires thinking differently about how leadership teams and governance bodies engage and how they operate. As illustrated on the next page:

- Leadership practices that need digitizing include direction setting and focused priorities enablement, executive sponsorship of key initiatives and organizational engagement.
- Employee engagement mechanisms that need digitization include all types of communication, global perspectives input and real-time feedback processes.

- Collaboration processes that need digitization include those related to training and knowledge transfer, those that enable more effective teamwork or create a Bias for Action.

At the core is simplifying, standardizing and optimizing the decision-making business process workflow, through the use of real-time collaboration platforms. Alas, the number and type of available software tools to do so are vast and the list keeps growing every day. A few examples include online team workspaces, interactive intranets, online meeting management, *Follow-the-Sun* strategic planning, project, program and portfolio management software, and online team engagement processes. Digital decision-making includes predictive analytics support based on the real-time dashboards, scorecards and other performance management variance data. It means abandoning INFORM as the basis for meetings and pivoting meetings to be either decision or issues based built on a firm-wide *Single Source of Truth* for plan, portfolio, project and program information.

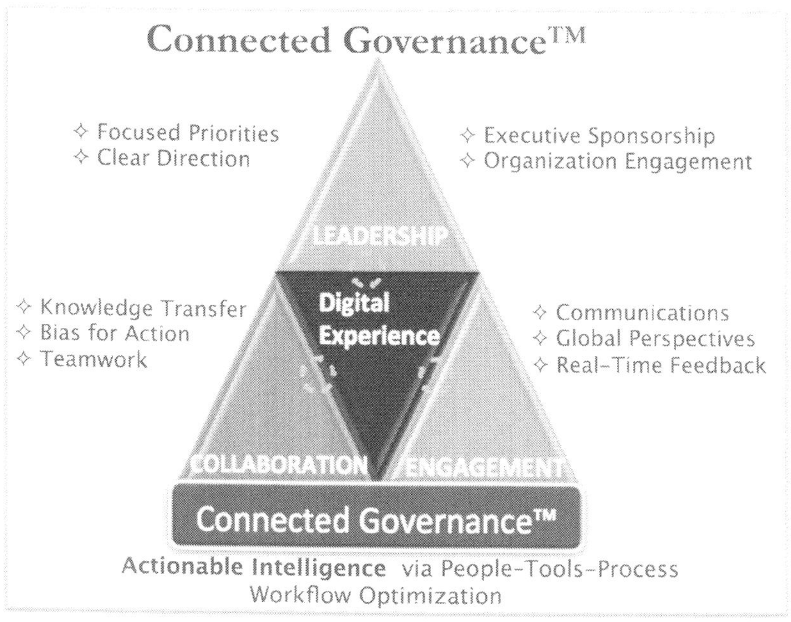

After having been involved with several large business model transformations, it is evident that there are five important governance workflows that need to be automated that are critical for Connected Governance™. They include:

- The digitization of leadership team meeting information in a user-friendly, branded way that includes continuous reminders as to the meeting mandate and success criteria. This would include items such as agendas, rolling calendars, attendance tracking, meeting minutes and recordings, program status updates, business scorecards, issues logs, decision logs, presentations, discussion forums and action item tracking.
- Digital meeting facilitation, which addresses proactively how meetings are conducted with real-time collaboration tools that enable *follow the sun* engagement, pre-meeting Q&A and voting designed to improve effectiveness, quality of conversation and support of non-native English-speaking participants.
- Open and transparent virtual results tracking including online, real-time scorecards, dashboards that capture and track status, action items with auto notification of activities such as Action Item due dates, decisions and issues that can be exported to other voting or prioritization online tools.
- Digital stakeholder management, including not just meeting participants, but all of those that are affected by the governance process including outreach, inform and feedback processes. Platforms exist today that allow real-time response visibility, and qualitative and quantitative questioning based on multi-media interactions. (audio, video, text, image etc.)
- Mechanisms that standardize, automate and optimize

workflow and enable transparent access to operational actionable intelligence across functions and even across enterprises (i.e. with channel partners and suppliers). In addition digital mechanisms that track the impact and effectiveness of the decisions made from a quality and cycle time perspective are also of value.

CONNECTED GOVERNANCE SUCCESS EXAMPLES

Below is a prototype of a digital meeting organizer, created for a large networking firm to drive leadership team meetings. On the left are the agenda item topics grouped into Top of Mind and Scorecard Summaries, Program Decision Requests, Discussion Topics, Issues Topics and a Learnings Update section. In the centre are all of the links needed for the meeting that are accessible in one place. These include attendance logs, rolling calendars, minutes and recordings of previous meetings, action and issues logs, copies of all

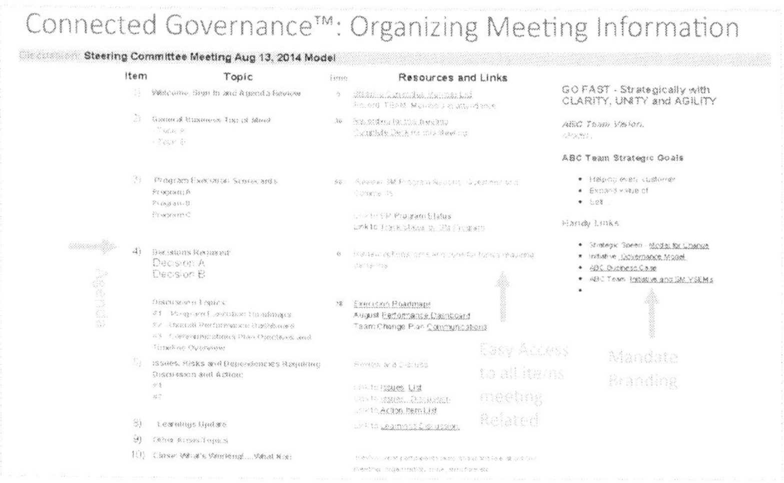

presentations, discussion forums, prioritized backlog lists, etc. On the right are placeholders for meeting *branding*, which could include the mandate, key objectives and other handy links of interest to the team. Engagement/collaboration areas also exist for each topic so that action items and issues can be captured in real time or questions posed and answers posted in advance.

BENEFITS OF CONNECTED GOVERNANCE™

The key benefits of this type of governance are many, but the highlights include:

- Data is entered ONCE and then re-purposed in many ways for many uses based on a *Single Source of Truth*.
- Less PowerPoint or Excel coordination is required and version control mistakes are minimized.
- More flexible reporting and improved efficiency in building reports, scorecards and dashboards improves decision-making cycle time.
- Improved *line of sight* clarity between personal, team and divisional work efforts and corporate strategies creates more time for staffs to engage in predictive-preemptive analysis rather than just coordination activities.
- Digitization processes enable direct and transparent access to information and to actionable intelligence by executive management to whatever level they desire. In addition, multi-level mechanisms are available for comments, discussions and input at all participating organizational levels, both cross functionally and globally.
- Download or publishing capability exists either via direct access or via online report form to online communities for team outreach.
- Unified commitment, teamwork and deepening global collaboration strengthens firm agility, communication, ideas exchange, knowledge transfer and *Best Practices* learning.

As shared by Davis, Frechette and Boswell from The Forum Corporation in their book, **Strategic Speed**, research shows that huge predictors of speedy strategy execution are four key leadership practices. We believe that these are also critical for Agile Strategy Execution. They include:

- Creating a **shared understanding of the overall business strategy** so that everyone on the team gains full understanding and buy-in of the external and internal business case for change. In addition, they understand the details of who, what, when, where and how of the strategy with opportunity, in a *catch-ball* way, to shape and adjust the execution roadmap.
- **Driving strategic initiatives** not just by sponsorship, but through regular *hands on* involvement launched with energy and ongoing leadership engagement through real-time reporting and commenting, with focus on identifying and removing the impediments to people making needed behavior changes, i.e. *Hands on the Steering Wheel*, so that course corrections are being made continuously.
- Direct **managing of culture and climate** and clarity on how it needs to change to become more aligned, accountable and agile through regular *temperature checks*, opportunities for open dialogue, and encouraging ownership, flexibility and confidence in making decisions as low in the hierarchy as possible.
- **Cultivating Experience** by enabling an environment that values continuous learning and improvement, encourages action and reflection and the sharing of insights, helps people to learn from experience and apply lessons quickly to emerging problems.

Davis, Frechette and Boswell have included in their book Strategic Speed, a series of assessment surveys for both individuals and leadership teams. Another that has been successfully used in setting the stage for Refresh/Transform meetings or large initiative kickoff session is their Strategic Speedometer Assessment. This exercise assesses the degree to which the organization or business unit is paying attention to the people factors of clarity, unity and agility. Any of these instruments can be easily turned into effective Impression Capture™ tools to assess an organization's current success in adopting these leadership practices and their overall skill level in enabling clarity, unity and agility. These are useful supplements to the Agile Strategy Execution Maturity Model assessment.

CONCLUSIONS AND KEY TAKEAWAYS

CONCLUSIONS

Our intent in this book has been to share over 60 years of combined experience as both strategy and execution practitioners and consultants to help revolutionize the HOW of strategy execution. Our hope is that along the way you better understand the challenges, the myths, and obstacles to effective strategy execution. We introduced the idea of an agile Strategy Execution Maturity Model™ that should help organizations assess where they are on an evolving scale in their own strategy execution maturity. We have drawn on many of the industry's *best practice* methodologies, approaches, tools, methods, processes, solutions and enablers both to provide both theoretical constructs along with some practical advice to aid in enabling your firm's strategy execution to become more agile. We expect that you now have an understanding of our Agile Strategy Execution Framework™ and believe that it will provide you with an effective construct to help organize the tools, processes and methods your company may currently be using to help enable easier deployment and improvement execution. In this way, the strategy-execution practitioner will have, at their fingertips, a systematic and workable way to approach, communicate, align and use effectively all of these various strategy execution processes, methods and techniques. As described at the beginning, creating the Agile Strategy Execution Framework™ came from reflecting how difficult strategy execution is and how generally miserable the track record has been over the last 15 years. We believe that more Agile Strategy Execution using techniques and yes – some software applications, so as to enable effective digitization of the entire workflow - will generate a multitude of benefits including:

- A powerful common taxonomy and methodology to describe strategic and tactical intent.
- Enabling the linkage of all strategies, execution priorities, detailed organization and department plans and tactics.
- Ensuring transparency and direct line-of-sight using a single framework that is accessible by all.
- Driving effective cross-functional communication, synchronization, feedback loops and information sharing with team involvement and buy-in.
- Encouraging real-time organization performance evaluation and governance with real-time course correction.
- Coordinating, refining and prioritizing work in real time with the appropriate adjustments to changing landscapes.
- Improved quality and cycle time in decision-making with faster Time-to-Value.
- A greater ability to anticipate and respond to change.

In summary, organizations will be aligned, accountable and much more responsive. As mentioned previously:

Being ALIGNED means that all employees have a strong feeling of ownership of strategy/execution steps/plans. It means improved communication or information sharing between individuals or business units responsible for strategy execution. It means that all components of strategy (objectives, initiatives and projects) are linked and coordinated.

Being ACCOUNTABLE means that there is clear communication, ownership and responsibility for execution decisions at all levels of the organization. It means greater understanding of the importance of variance performance management and of being data-driven. It means line of sight virtual ownership of strategy and how it gets executed up and down and across the organization.

Being RESPONSIVE means proactive and predictive management of a changing marketplace and customer needs, based on an environment that supports continuous improvement and course correction. It means an improved ability to manage change effectively.

However, the truth is that initial plans last as long as the first contact with reality. This means that adaptation and the ability to pivot and respond to changing landscapes in a positive way must be frequent and result in ongoing realignment. All employees, not just the leadership team, need to be engaged and involved in all steps of the strategy execution process including the essence of collaboration i.e. creating, deploying and refining.

KEY TAKEAWAYS

Key takeaways and our recommendations for practical next steps include:

- Evaluating your organization using our Agile Strategy Execution Maturity Model™ and assessing the gaps between where you are and where you want your organization to be.
- Deciding which areas to work on first, where you can get the best traction, and generate some good Quick-Wins in a reasonable timeframe.
- Using the Agile Strategy Execution™ as a guide for organizational and operating model transformation as you drive alignment, accountability and responsiveness.
- Considering the use of Impression Capture™ techniques to create good baseline assessments to calibrate collective understanding of how well individuals and leaders are doing in building bench strength capabilities such as Strategic Speed's™ leadership people factors.
- Periodically evaluating your organization's Agile Strategy Execution™ progress and refining implementation plans as needed.
- Creating an environment where all can experiment and learn from what works and what doesn't and celebrate success frequently both big and small.

All of the protagonists, whose stories we shared at the beginning of this narrative, and many of our colleagues and supporters have experimented and/or used various aspects of our Agile Strategy Execution Framework™ with good success. However, as with all journeys there may be some road bumps and potholes along the way. What makes our community of Agile Strategy Execution practitioners special, though, is our collective willingness to share both the good and the challenges. To help in this effort we've created a public LinkedIn Group (Agile Strategy Execution). Please feel free to join and share your experiences.

APPENDIX A - TECHNIQUES

Many of the illustrations presented in the main body of this book have been and continue to be used by a number of our clients, including the three protagonists discussed at the beginning. Each has chosen different dimensions to work on and frequently different aspects of the same dimension. All of them had to reflect on the potential enabling or disabling impacts of their own corporate culture and assess their degree of commitment to Connected Governance™. Some have made these transitions easily, others have not, and it continues to be an ongoing journey of reflection and discovery. In this chapter are a number of techniques and templates that we have found to be useful and worthy of consideration.

MATURITY MODEL FOR AGILE STRATEGY EXECUTION ENABLEMENT

In our view, Agile Strategy Execution is an approach *"that enables an organization, function or team to translate their strategy into an execution reality that is 'Aligned, Accountable and Responsive', thereby delivering timely value in a way that contributes to the achievement of identified goals or business outcomes."* We define business outcomes as typically being one of five types: growing revenue, cost savings through more efficient and effective internal processes, improved customer satisfaction, risk reduction or enabling competitive advantage through market or customer differentiation.

Also, as mentioned previously, if a firm is ALIGNED, it means that all components of strategy (goals and objectives, strategic priorities, initiative investment portfolios, Run-the-Business (RTB) activities, tactics and other programs/projects) must be linked, coordinated, and cascaded through the organization, both vertically and horizontally. If an organization, function or team is ACCOUNTABLE, it means that all employees involved in strategy execution are committed to what is being created with direct and visible line of sight, and can see clearly the interconnectedness and their role and value contribution. If the strategy execution process is RESPONSIVE, it means that initial plans can adapt to evolving or changing internal and external landscapes in a way that results in frequent and ongoing realignment and re-prioritization of emphasis and resources. It requires a decision-making process based on data-driven critical assessments of performance with public views and common definitions of all measurements and analytical processes.

But how does an organization know if their strategy execution process is aligned, accountable and responsive enough? The easiest way to find out is to conduct a maturity model assessment. Assessment via a maturity model is not a new construct. Carnegie Melon University created one of the earliest ones that they called Capability Maturity Model Integration (CMMI). According to Wikipedia, CMMI was originally used as *"a training and appraisal program and service used to guide process improvement across a project division or an entire organization."*

STAGES OF MATURITY EVOLUTION

Though the original CMMI approach worked with five stages of maturity evolution, we've consolidated that into four key stages: namely Task Oriented, Managed, Integrated and Optimized. Each stage involves an assessment based on four key parameters including a review of who is involved with the planning process, what tools and techniques support it, how strategic investments are made, and lastly the level and type of stakeholder involvement. We've developed these parameters based on more than 60 combined years of experience in trying to help firms strengthen their strategy and execution processes from planning to project and program management to strategic investment portfolio management. Specifically:

Task Oriented: If a company is task oriented, generally a yearly strategic planning process is completed at the organization level, usually beginning with a management team offsite of some kind. Such team building meetings include both work and play time, whether it's golf, a nice meal, or attending a play. The process is designed so that leaders can get to know each other in somewhat of a non-work setting. Using readily available internal and external assessment data with some ad hoc planning activities at the function or department level, most strategic investments are designed to build a new capability or focus the organization in some way. Examples could include a new sales model, or supply chain optimization program or a marketing campaign to support a new product or service launch for which the departments involved are given incremental funding to drive. Department leaders are expected to lead execution, which generally occurs in organizational silos with little cross-functional interaction. The overall plan and strategy are communicated only to key leaders, rarely publicly and if so, only high-level aspirational goals and related strategies are shared. Each functional leader is expected to execute on their part of the collective execution *To Do* list.

Managed Oriented: In this scenario, strategy execution is a much more formal process that provides oversight to both organizational and function specific activities in some way with active stakeholder participation. Annual planning meetings are usually front-ended by a much more formal and proactive external data collection process, such as external competitive and market analyses, as well as Technology-Social-Political-Economic (TSPE) trends assessments, polling or temperature readings. An internal performance assessment process takes place usually based on broad financial and other performance metrics (such as a Balanced Scorecard), which help connect expected outcomes to the execution plan. Formal strategy assessment tools such as SWOT (Strengths-Weaknesses-Opportunities-Threats), Kano customer satisfaction driver, or Force Field (hindering and helping factors) analysis are also sometimes included. Specific funding is set aside for key strategic investments that are monitored and measured centrally or locally with specific expected outcomes and performance measurements defined. Sometimes cross-functional interlocks take place to drive internal alignment. The overall organizational strategic plan is more frequently communicated at the aspirational level, but detailed operational plans are still left at the functional level, though sometimes a more formal management review of functional plans may take place. Staff allegiance is generally to the functional plan, not to the overall organizational strategic plan.

Integrated Oriented: In this scenario, significant effort is undertaken to coordinate and integrate specific strategies and plans with both external data and internal performance results at both the organizational and departmental level. Automation is introduced so that there is a *Single Source of Truth* for key project and program information, performance metrics and outcomes. Strategic investments are managed and monitored as an ROI/Value based portfolio and expected to contribute to the achievement of desired business outcomes. In addition, execution priorities are clearly mapped to projects, programs and key Run-the-Business (RTB) programs. All stakeholders are proactively involved with group decision-making. Functions are expected and incentivized to support *collective* strategies as well as their own prioritized activities. Functions are more easily able to see how their work efforts contribute to both the functional and the organizational strategic plan.

Optimized Oriented: If an organization is optimized oriented, both strategy and execution are ongoing and in real-time. External shifts and internal performance data are monitored on an ongoing basis and are used to refresh and transform organizational and function-specific strategies and tactics. Strategic investment portfolios are managed more aggressively with periodic *Stop-Start-Continue* assessments if expected results aren't met. Stakeholders are rewarded based on both individual and team execution accomplishments. Key RTB activities tracking also move online.

Each of our three Agile Strategy Execution pillars is then assessed with respect to a set of behaviours characteristic of each stage. For the sake of completion, we've added a strategy creation pillar so that practitioners can evaluate originating strategic planning processes if needed. However, for the purposes of our discussion in this narrative, we assumed that effective processes exist and that the overall strategic plan has been created. Below is a table illustrating the characteristics of each pillar across each maturity model stage with a summary description below.

Agile Strategy Maturity Matrix™

	Creation	Aligned	Accountable	Responsive
Optimized	Ongoing real-time assessment & refinement of org./area strategies based on inter. & external factors.	Plan refinements trigger org. wide notification/ discussion /corrective actions with all affected areas/ owners... real time.	Real time org/area KPI's visible & acted upon. Metrics variances lead to real-time discussion/refinement for area plans, budgets & actions.	Institutionalized agile strategy execution process in place. Agile processes & culture change embedded in organization.
Integrated	Integration of org./ area: plans, external data & internal performance.	Transparent, real-time coordination between area plans. Cross-area initiatives coordinated between teams. Tactics/projects aligned & linked to objectives.	Org. & area metrics linked/ cascaded to area objectives. Variances reported with real-time actions. Coordinated portfolio-based initiative funding.	Area real time sprint decision making & retrospectives conducted within/between areas. KPI & issue triggers drive plan reassessment & backlog management.
Managed	Formal process for: org/ area plan development. Use of formal internal & external focused tools & stakeholder participation.	Formal process to align/ cascade Org. & area plans vertically and horizontally. Employee tactics incorporated into area plans.	Resources allocated/managed for key initiatives & tactics. Plan progress regularly measured & reported. Variances to plan initiates corrective actions.	Areas conduct periodic scrums. Plan performance measured with corrective actions assigned. Backlog used to plan next set of work (sprint).
Task Oriented	Yearly organization & selected dept plans developed, using available data	Selected area plans and activities aligned and linked to organization plans.	Org metrics & area indicators are quantified/reviewed for selected initiatives/areas. Area key initiative funding.	Selected areas. link objectives to activities with scheduled reviews. Selected objectives/ tactics visibly managed.

As indicated previously, a critical part of enabling Agile Strategy Execution is to ensure that all components of strategy including goals/objectives, strategic priorities, key initiatives, programs and projects and key RTB tactics are linked, coordinated and cascaded through the organization, both vertically and horizontally to both direct and extended stakeholders.

ALIGNMENT PILLAR MATURITY EVOLUTION

This ALIGNMENT at the TASK stage usually involves only those functions or departments that are directly involved with the organizational strategic plan and accomplished usually on an ad hoc basis. When MANAGED, there is a formal process put in place that drives vertical and horizontal interlock and in some cases, employee activities and tactics are incorporated. At the INTEGRATED stage, the alignment and linkage of organizational and functional plans occur in real-time with all key RTB activities and tactics, as well as strategic project and program portfolios also linked and aligned. Information concerning the level and type of cross-functional initiatives linkage and alignment is clearly visible.

At the OPTIMIZED stage, incremental or dramatic refinements to organization and function-specific plans or RTB activities and tactics trigger real-time online organization-wide notifications, discussions, reviews, etc., with corrective action redirection setting involving all affected functions and even potential *subject-matter experts* (SME's) lower in the organization.

ACCOUNTABILITY PILLAR MATURITY EVOLUTION

Another pillar of Agile Strategy Execution is the driving of ACCOUNTABILITY through the organization. When TASK ORIENTED, this involves formal scheduled INFORM-based reviews of selected initiatives or functions. Such reviews typically outline accomplishments, challenges, focus areas, quantified key performance indicators and any needed get-well plans and customer/market updates. Each is assessed individually with no cross-function analytics. At the MANAGED stage, formal INFORM-based reviews take place to assess progress-to-plan of all operational plans with resources managed and allocated for all strategic initiatives and RTB activities and tactics. Key performance indicator variances definitions are formally established, measured and results reviewed. Formal follow-up corrective action or tiger-team assessments to determine necessary corrective action are proactively managed and reported on.

When operating at the INTEGRATED Stage, all organization and functional key performance indicators are visible in real-time and are linked and cascaded to all functional plans, strategic initiatives and key RTB activities and tactics in such a way that all teams have clear line of site online as to which strategic priorities they are contributing to or for which goals their work efforts are driving achievement. Variances are reported and reviewed and corrective action taken on a more frequent basis (monthly or quarterly basis) and coordinated across functions where appropriate, including *Stop-Start-Continue* decision-making, pushed as low in the organization as possible. Senior leadership focus is on cross-functional risk assessment and mitigation, and issue resolution. When OPTIMIZED, KPI variances are visible and acted upon in real-time based on real-time discussion and refinement of all affected functions, plans, budgets and RTB activities and tactics.

RESPONSIVENESS PILLAR MATURITY EVOLUTION ACROSS EACH STAGE

When operating with a high degree of RESPONSIVENESS at the TASK stage, strategic initiatives, key Run-the-Business activities/programs engage in either periodic or post program/project or process assessments (PPA) so as to uncover and share *lessons learned* amongst involved function-specific teams and reporting structures. When in the MANAGED stage, agility is driven through open leader-driven proactive cultivation, harnessing and sharing not just *lessons learned* but experience with lots of time for reflection on an individual or team basis with opportunities for experimentation. At the INTEGRATED stage, formal real-time plan updates based on day-to-day *triggers* drive reprioritization and scheduling of work/activity backlog at the individual, team, and function levels through *Cadence Decisions* and *Innovation Bets* that cultivate team reflection, experimentation and knowledge transfer. When in the

OPTIMIZED stage, real-time experience cultivation happens at the organizational level with focus on cross-functional *Cadence Decisions* and *Innovation Bets.* In addition, thematic *triggers* drive reassessment of key strategic plan assumptions, reprioritization of portfolio program/project backlog and organizational strategy course correction, as well as cultivate cross-organizational team reflection, experimentation and knowledge transfer.

CURRENT STATE OF MATURITY AND GAP COMPARISONS

Once comfortable with your understanding of both the pillars and the evolution stages, it's time to put them together and ascertain not just where your organization is today, but where it would like to be in the future. Below is the maturity chart with the red (solid) circles marking where the firm currently is today and the green (dotted) circles indicating where the firm wishes to be in the future.

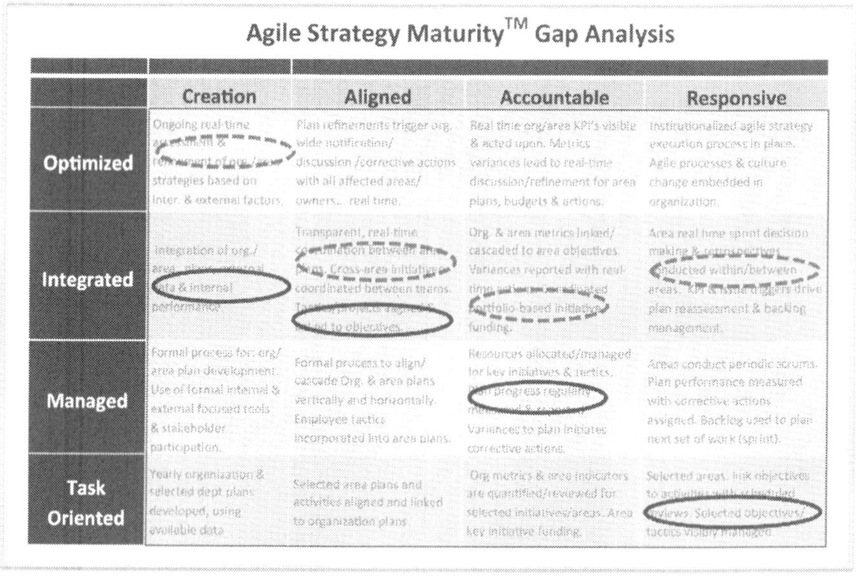

Agile Strategy Maturity™ Gap Analysis

	Creation	Aligned	Accountable	Responsive
Optimized	Ongoing real-time assessment & refinement of org./area strategies based on inter. & external factors.	Plan refinements trigger org. wide notification/ discussion /corrective actions with all affected areas/ owners.. real time.	Real time org/area KPI's visible & acted upon. Metrics variances lead to real-time discussion/refinement for area plans, budgets & actions.	Institutionalized agile strategy execution process in place. Agile processes & culture change embedded in organization.
Integrated	Integration of org./ area plans, external data & internal performance.	Transparent, real-time coordination between area plans. Cross-area initiatives coordinated between teams. Tactics/projects aligned & linked to objectives.	Org. & area metrics linked/ cascaded to area objectives. Variances reported with real-time [illegible] Portfolio-based initiative funding.	Area real time sprint decision making & retrospectives conducted within/between areas. KPI & issue triggers drive plan reassessment & backlog management.
Managed	Formal process for: org/ area plan development. Use of formal internal & external focused tools & stakeholder participation.	Formal process to align/ cascade Org. & area plans vertically and horizontally. Employee tactics incorporated into area plans.	Resources allocated/managed for key initiatives & tactics. Plan progress regularly [illegible] Variances to plan initiates corrective actions.	Areas conduct periodic scrums. Plan performance measured with corrective actions assigned. Backlog used to plan next set of work (sprint).
Task Oriented	Yearly organization & selected dept plans developed, using available data	Selected area plans and activities aligned and linked to organization plans.	Org metrics & area indicators are quantified/reviewed for selected initiatives/areas. Area key initiative funding.	Selected areas link objectives to activities with scheduled reviews. Selected objectives/ tactics visibly managed.

Most organizations operate today at the TASK and MANAGED stage, and those well versed in strategic planning *Best Practices* probably score reasonably well in driving accountable vertical alignment.

However, without proactive, leader-driven experience cultivation, it is difficult to enable a responsive environment. This is especially true when protagonists are drowning in PowerPoint presentations and Excel-based assessments. Unfortunately, an effective transition to the INTEGRATED and OPTIMIZED stages requires moving online to the proactive use of real-time collaboration tools, project, program, portfolio and planning software applications, which many organizations find challenging. It also requires serious re-engineering of governance and decision-making processes up and down the organization, especially for those who operate globally.

Agile Strategy Maturity Gap Analysis

Maturity	Creation	Aligned	Accountable	Responsive
Optimized				
Integrated				
Managed				
Task				

In summary, our Agile Strategy Execution Maturity Model™ assessment process involves answering a set of questions capturing both where you think your organization or department is today vs. where you'd like your organization or department to be in the future. What is critical is making the first step so as to have an accurate baseline. In order to do that, it's important to conduct an honest assessment of where one's team, function and/or organization is today and where it aspires to be in the future, both short term and long term. In order to help advance this effort, we've created a formal assessment process, whereby not only can you assess your own organization's stage in our Agile Strategy Execution Model™, but you can also see where you are relative to all other organizations of a similar size and geographic scope. On the previous page is an example of the results of our current survey population of firms who have completed the maturity model assessment. As can be seen, there are significant gaps between CURRENT and DESIRED states for all participants. Interestingly enough, it is especially critical in the Responsive pillar. This suggests that efforts to drive accountability should be where most firms need to begin their improvement work. The next step would be for strategy execution practitioners to review the Agile Strategy Execution Framework™ and ascertain how to improve accountability in the dimension of their choosing.

If you'd like to take the test for either your team or your firm, please feel free to reach out and email us at info@agilestrategymanager.com

DIGITIZING AGILE STRATEGY EXECUTION: AGILE STRATEGY MANAGER®

Agile Strategy Manager® is a software platform from Y-Change, based in Pleasanton, CA that drives coordinated accountability and decision-making by enabling organizations to integrate, align and manage all strategic and tactical, information online. Departments or teams can easily organize, manage and link their execution programs and projects to functional or cross-functional strategies, objectives, initiatives and tactics throughout the organization. Executives and managers can easily create and update all information and performance metrics, with a simple double click.

The Agile Integrated Strategy Application Suite has three main components and a number of key features outlined below.

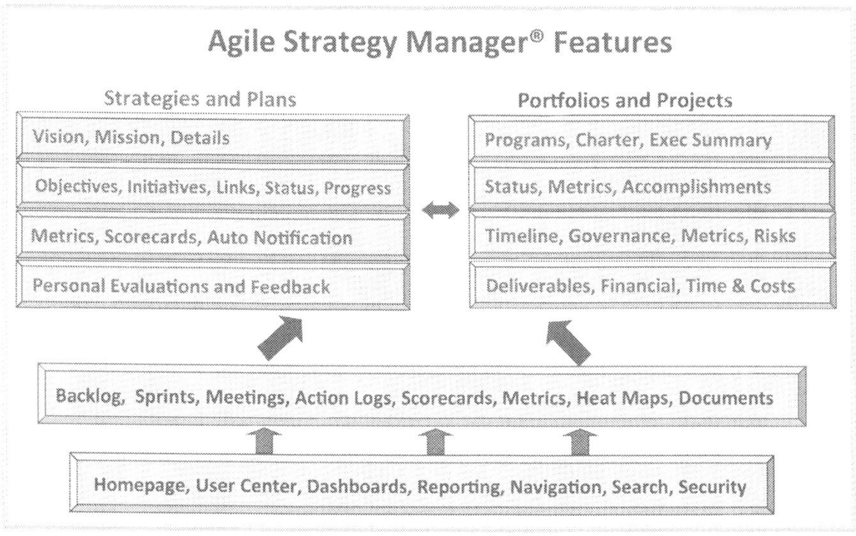

PLANNING MODULE

Firstly, is a planning module called the Agile Strategy and Initiative Cascade that enables visual direct line-of-sight from strategies to initiatives, programs and projects. High-level views of all aspects of strategic, tactical and performance management information can be integrated, aligned and managed from one location. Key features include the ability to:

- Review and collaborate on strategy details, scorecards and links to other department plans and internally stored documents.
- Get automated or double click updates of your team's progress with auto-generated metrics charts and scorecards.
- Look Ahead/Back enables visibility review/reference information from prior years for input into current or future years.
- Assign, coordinate and follow up on meetings and action items. Automated emails can be generated for past due items, change of status or owners.
- Use your current organization's process, including Hoshin, OKR's, MBO (Management by Objectives), or VSE (Vision-Strategy-Execution). Information is automatically displayed and editable in both department & personal views.

PROJECT, PROGRAM AND PORTFOLIO MANAGEMENT

Secondly, is a set of project, program and portfolio management features that facilitates the alignment, tracking and team collaboration on the progress of multiple projects from one simple interface. Projects can be grouped into programs and into various strategic investment portfolios and then analyzed from each of these varied perspectives. This is especially useful when managing projects that cut across department boundaries (i.e. Six Sigma), or are part of broader global or corporate initiatives. Specifically, its project and program collaboration features enable decentralized teams to align, track, manage, and account for their progress. Executives and managers can select, plan, manage and track a portfolio's lifecycle from idea to execution, and therefore make decisions with a much higher degree of confidence.

Everyone in the cascade has easy access to all of the information they need including Gantt charts, risks, deliverables, phase status, heat maps and custom dashboards, as well as high-level summaries so as to understand who is doing what and how their work strategically aligns to meet organizational business goals. This level of visibility, including both top-down and lateral perspectives, ensures that teams are working on the right things, at the right time. The rules engine allows for quick phase gate approvals, emails, and prioritizing of projects for selection or re-sizing. In this way, an organization can easily view the metrics of their portfolio, as well as the specific objectives and initiatives that they are supporting.

PERFORMANCE MANAGEMENT REPORTING

Thirdly, are a set of agile performance management reporting features that enable the creation of dashboards and scorecards at the program, project or portfolio level, including strategy-to-project, project-to-program and portfolio-to-program views. These reports can be tailored to the individual needs of each leader and then saved, emailed, printed or exported to Excel, Word or PDF formats as needed. With simple *double click* online editing, enabling real-time updates *on-the-fly* is easy so that all reports can quickly be kept up to date.

KEY BENEFITS OF AGILE STRATEGY MANAGER®

Overall key benefits include:

- Agile Integration of all Strategy to Project information in one location that is easily accessible.
- Customizable Cascade Reports that can view all linked strategies, initiatives and projects on one screen. Simple double click editing makes updating information in the Sprint meeting effortless.
- Customized reporting of programs, projects and even portfolios to fit business objectives and the ability to quickly gain insight into how programs and projects are enabling achievement of top-level strategic objectives.

Reminder: Most of the illustrations in the Agile Strategy Execution Framework™ section (the six dimensions) were generated using client data from the Agile Strategy Manager® Digital application. Data was altered to preserve client confidentiality.

CLOUD COLLABORATION PLATFORM: GROUPMIND EXPRESS

GroupMind™, based in California, is a flexible set of cloud-based integrated collaboration tools that support planning and change processes across functional and geographic boundaries.

Based on over 30 years of practical experience, facilitating thousands of meetings, surveys and organizational assessments, planning sessions, 360 assessments, change management processes, and learning engagements, GroupMind™ was originally

designed as a way for people to work together by sharing their thinking and their information through participative planning processes. Today its visual tools allow many participants to rapidly input honest thinking, set priorities, share documents, and make decisions and track initiatives. GroupMind™ is best used for supporting collaborative, culture change and governance aspects of Agile Strategy Execution including:

- Initial and Refresh/Transform Strategic planning dimensions.
- Cadence Decisions and Innovation Bets Planning.
- Managing governance and leadership interactions.
- Culture and other types of organizational assessments.
- Employee engagement for all types of change adoption.
- 360 Job Performance Evaluations.
- Learning and Development.

A wide variety of mechanisms are available in GroupMind™ to move teams through a logical process of identifying possibilities, prioritizing, aligning, planning, managing initiatives, and ultimately presenting strategic plans and ideas in a form that drives organizational learning. At each level, tools can be integrated to leverage data in various ways. Group convergence starts when respondents reflect on and discuss the range of thought that is now made visible.

STEPS TO DRIVE COLLABORATION EFFECTIVENESS

There are three key steps to drive effectiveness of this kind of collaboration.

The first and most important is to efficiently find out what people really think. Managers, change agents and initiative owners do better when they know what people really think. Honest information is a starting place for change to take hold and stick. GroupMind™ levels the playing field for candid communications. For example, the Impression Capture™ survey tool enables participants, anonymously or not as the team desires, to share their key concerns or clarify what isn't clear from previous meetings or communications. Results are available instantaneously showing histograms, statistics, and comment sets all in one place. Other types of survey instruments can be created and distributed quickly, with a link included in an email from an email client or from GroupMind GroupMail.™ This kind of data gathering allows an organization to leverage more effectively its collective intelligence and realize in a direct way that a team's collective intelligence is greater than the sum of its individual parts.

Secondly, are mechanisms that allow teams to make sense of all of the ideas generated and create alignment. For example, teams can virtually discuss or brainstorm critical problems or share ideas or track critical items and then move the master list of items into a selection of voting tools. These voting tools drive group prioritization and decision-making in ways that help focus discussions and most importantly, accelerate alignment for initiatives that will have the desired results. The continuous automatic documentation of the process is especially valuable for those unable to attend, as they can quickly and easily participate and catch up. There are even notification processes that can automatically let participants know when updates are made to the process. A *Follow Me* feature enables *guided browsing* so that participants can assign browser control to the Leader, who can navigate and then bring all linked members to that page.

Thirdly, is the fact that meeting governance can be transformed from boring INFORM constructs to highly engaged interactions for planning, creating buy-in, and making decisions. Meeting templates allow the integration of PowerPoint presentations, converted to SlideShows, questions and comments, interactive decision support and built-in feedback all in one place that are easily archived and accessed by participants at any time in the future. For example, rather than waiting until the end of an INFORM presentation, the GroupMind™ SlideShow tool allows for the gathering of questions and comments relevant to each specific slide, in the moment. Post meeting feedback requests can be built into the meeting process flow, so as to get an immediate feel for how it went and what could be done differently next time. Pre and post meeting information for standing governance bodies can be enabled in a single location for easy access to rolling agendas, attendance tracking, meeting minutes, recordings, action items, discussion narratives, scorecards and issues tracking.

Last, are a set of GroupMind™ templates such as SWOT analysis, Force Field, Balanced Scorecard and Organizational Assessments. This kind of collaboration is especially useful in situations where hot issues need an equal playing field and robust decision-making or where language barriers may exist. Notes are available immediately, with no paper charts to transcribe. Issues are captured in the participant's own words; everyone can review the input at any time.

UNLEASHING THE POWER OF THE GROUPMIND™

Today's business leaders can't afford to move on a new idea or action plan without the creative collaboration of everyone responsible for executing the plan. As Ken Ketch, President of GroupMind™ has said, *"Change succeeds best when executives take steps to ensure the buy-in of their whole team. Leaders need new ways to rapidly garner honest feedback from team members, from interdependent teams, and from suppliers and customers so they can find out 'if the emperor is wearing no clothes,' thus avoiding costly mistakes."* All of this must be accomplished very quickly within narrow time constraints. These tasks are challenging in the best of circumstances, and are much more difficult to achieve when teams are geographically dispersed.

ENABLING ACTIONABLE INTELLIGENCE: (Q2E™)

According to Dave O'Callaghan, a Q2E™ key advisor and channel expert, corporate agility is the *"ability for a firm to change its position efficiently, and requires the integration across functions using the combination of balance, coordination, speed, reflexes, strength, and endurance. To achieve corporate agility, firms need to have all functions aligned on execution, and focus on eliminating costly, duplicative work."*

Q2E™ provides real-time actionable intelligence at an operational level, across functions and enterprises. With Q2E™, you can engage your work ecosystem, measure what matters, and scale. Through the implementation of this user-friendly, cloud-based SaaS offering, firms can standardize their processes, automate the work, and optimize the use of people, processes, and applications to get the work done. Progress can be measured and reported and ROI assessed across functions and enterprises in a way that enables ultimate accountability.

APPENDIX B - TEMPLATES

1. Maturity Model Summary Assessment
2. Hoshin Planning Template, A-1 Matrix
3. OKR Template
4. Wave Thinking Template
5. QFD Matrix
6. Agile Strategic Systems Thinking Template
7. SKEPTIC Environmental Scan Template
8. Meeting Cadence Template
9. Refresh-Transform Process Workflow
10. Culture, Employee Engagement, Leadership Practices and Change Impact Assessments

Agile Strategy Maturity Matrix™

	Creation	Aligned	Accountable	Responsive
Optimized	Ongoing real-time assessment & refinement of org./area strategies based on inter. & external factors.	Plan refinements trigger org. wide notification/ discussion /corrective actions with all affected areas/ owners... real time.	Real time org/area KPI's visible & acted upon. Metrics variances lead to real-time discussion/refinement for area plans, budgets & actions.	Institutionalized agile strategy execution process in place. Agile processes & culture change embedded in organization.
Integrated	Integration of org./ area: plans, external data & internal performance.	Transparent, real-time coordination between area plans. Cross-area initiatives coordinated between teams. Tactics/projects aligned & linked to objectives.	Org. & area metrics linked/ cascaded to area objectives. Variances reported with real-time actions. Coordinated portfolio-based initiative funding.	Area real time sprint decision making & retrospectives conducted within/between areas. KPI & issue triggers drive plan reassessment & backlog management.
Managed	Formal process for: org/ area plan development. Use of formal internal & external focused tools & stakeholder participation.	Formal process to align/ cascade Org. & area plans vertically and horizontally. Employee tactics incorporated into area plans.	Resources allocated/managed for key initiatives & tactics. Plan progress regularly measured & reported. Variances to plan initiates corrective actions.	Areas conduct periodic scrums. Plan performance measured with corrective actions assigned. Backlog used to plan next set of work (sprint).
Task Oriented	Yearly organization & selected dept plans developed, using available data	Selected area plans and activities aligned and linked to organization plans.	Org metrics & area indicators are quantified/reviewed for selected initiatives/areas. Area key initiative funding.	Selected areas. link objectives to activities with scheduled reviews. Selected objectives/ tactics visibly managed.

HOSHIN PLANNING TEMPLATE, A-1 MATRIX

Hoshin: Policy Deployment X Matrix

Company: ____________ Departments: ____________ Date: ______ Rev # ____

1 2 3 4 5 6 7 8 9 10

<<<Links>>>

Level 2 Initiatives

Level 2 Objectives

Metrics/ Programs

Top Level Objectives

<<<Links>>>

1 2 3 4

1 2 3 4

1 2 3 4 5 6 7 8 9

Resources

New Names

New Names

New Names

New Names

RACI

Responsible
Accountable
Consult
Inform

Objectives and Key Results (OKR) Template

Person __________________ Department: __________________ Date: _______ Rev # ___

	Weekly Progress				Month:		Month:		Month:	
Objective & Key Result	Current Status: R,Y,G,OH	Comments	% Complete	OKR Score	Attain-ment	OKR Score	Attain-ment	OKR Score	Attain-ment	OKR Score
Objective: 1.1:										
1.1.										
1.2.										
1.3.										
1.4										
Objective: 2:										
1.1.										
1.2.										
1.3.										
1.4										
Objective:3:										
1.1.										
1.2.										
1.3.										
1.4										
Objective: 4:										
1.1.										
1.2.										
1.3.										
1.4										

Wave Thinking℠ – Powering a *Breakthrough Sprint*℠

(Source: Forthcoming book titled *Rock Your Industry* by Jim Bandrowski, *RockYourIndustry.com*)

Breakthrough Wave℠ (Summary)			Innovation Potential*				Strategic Action Plan	
***Breakthrough Opportunity Areas*℠** (Unmet or Unknown Needs)	**Creative Leaps** (Wild Ideas)	**Breakthrough Concepts** (Potentially Feasible Solutions)	Attract-iveness (H,M,L) H = High	Feasi-bility (H,M,L) M = Medium	Synergy (H,M,L) L = Low	Timing (S,M,L) Short, Medium, or Long	**User Test Feedback** (Iterations of Prototypes, User Tests, and Feedback)	***Execution Excellence*℠ Plan**

***Definitions:** Attractiveness—To market and company. Feasibility—Will it work? Synergy—Aligns with our other strategies. Timing—Short, Medium, or Long term until revenue.

QFD: HOUSE OF QUALITY (Simplified A-1 Matrix)

WHAT vs. HOW

Value	Relationship Strenght
9	High
3	Medium
1	Low

				How's									Customer Analysis				
				1	2	3	4	5	6	7	8	9	Requirements Planning				
			Statement Relative Importance									What Vs. How Weighted Av.	Cust 1:	Cust 2:	Cust 3:	Cust 4:	What vs. Customer Weighted Avg.
	#	WHAT'S		How's relative weight									Customer Relative Weight				
Statements	1																
	2																
	3																
	4																
	5																
	6																
	7																
	8																
	9																
	10																
	11																
	12																
	13																
		Total How relative weight															

SYSTEMS THINKING PLANNING TEMPLATE

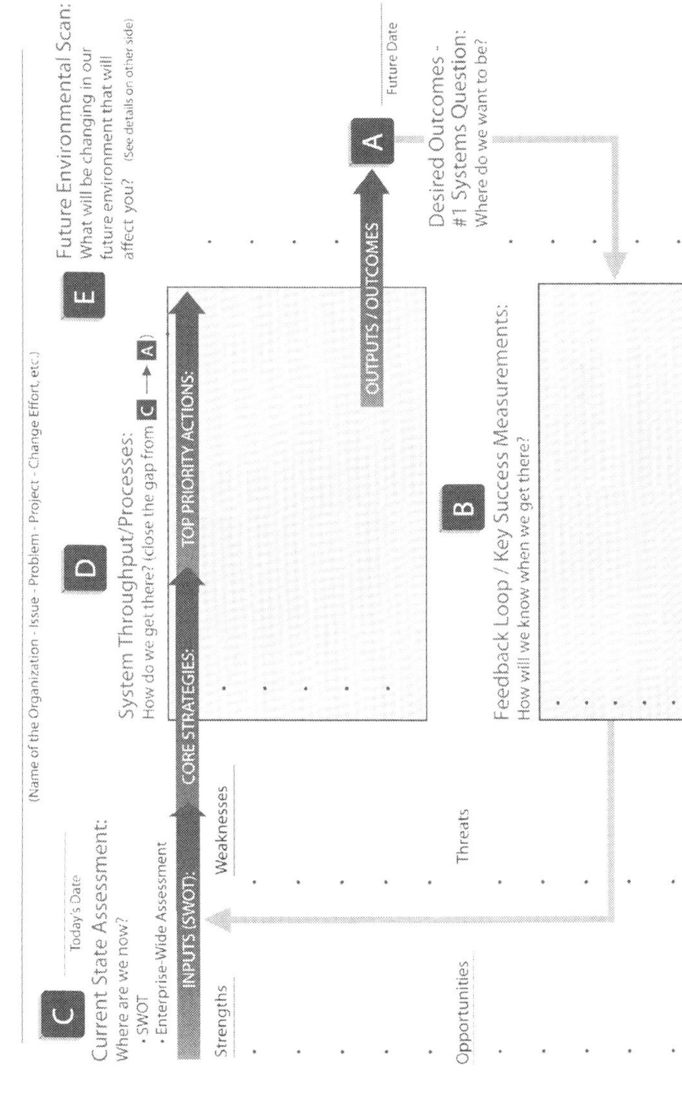

SKEPTIC ENVIRONMENTAL SCAN TEMPLATE

SKEPTIC Future EXTERNAL Environmental Scanning / Trends

List the 5-10 environmental trends - projections - opportunities - threats facing us over the life of our plan:

S Socio-Demographics (People / Society):

K Competition / Substitutes:

E Economics:

E Ecology (Including Natural Disasters):

P Political / Regulatory:

T Technical:

I Industry / Suppliers:

C Customer / Citizens:

MEETING CADENCE TEMPLATE

Agile Governance Cadence Template

Dimension	Purpose	Yearly	Quarterly	Monthly	Weekly	Daily	Responsible
Plans & Metrics	Translate objectives into area plans & metrics						
Align & Link	Align and link goals, strategies & operating plans						
Real-Time Updates	Drive real-time plan updates based on day-to-day triggers for prioritized backlog						
Cadence Decisions	Ensure appropriate resourcing & course correcting solutions to manage and prioritize backlog						Leaders
							Managers
							Work Teams
Innovation Bets	Identify and assess opportunities for innovation						

REFRESH OR TRANSFORM MEETING PROCESS WORKFLOW

As mentioned previously, the purpose of the Refresh or Transform dimension is to proactively reassess the current *deliberate* strategy in a formal way. Below is an example of a useful three-stage facilitated workflow that can be used to guide such meetings.

SITUATION ANALYSIS

- Existing Strategy & Direction
- Today's Value Proposition and Positioning
- Current Segmentation Strategy (products, markets, channels)
- Management Expectations
- Competitive Situation Update
- Customer/Partner Satisfaction & other Metrics Updates
- Current "As Is" Programs and Project Activities including status reports, metrics, timelines, deliverables
- New Ideas and Directions
- Top Issues, Concerns and Roadblocks

BRAINSTORMING QUESTIONS

Positioning

- Where have we been successful & why?
- Where have we been unsuccessful & why?
- What is it that we on balance do better than our competitors?
- What is it that our competitors on balance do better than us?
- If we had unlimited money, time and talent how would we reshape the jungle?
- What are our strengths and weaknesses?
- What new skills do we need to acquire? By When? How?
- What threatens us from making much progress? (culture, business and/or operating models)

Assessment of Risk

- What are the key strategic assumptions we are currently making about this aspect of the business?
- What are the top 4-6 issues that if we don't address it won't matter what else we do?

- What 5-6 key decisions require detailed evaluation, participation, concentration and energy from the team?
- What qualitative market or customer shifts must be considered?
- What are the risks associated with those shifts?
- What type of quantitative measures exists to evaluate those shifts?

DECISION-MAKING

- Revisit the high level mission and vision
- Determine key short term & long term goals & objectives
- Revisit key assumptions that have been made that frame the plan
- Clarify needed revisions to strategies to attain goals
- Determine specific programs or key efforts needed to execute on each strategy
- Determine prioritized list of issues, roadblocks and dependencies
- Identify the 5-6 most critical activities that must be done to address each outstanding issue? What resources are needed? By Whom? When?

CULTURE, EMPLOYEE ENGAGEMENT, LEADERSHIP PRACTICES, CHANGE IMPACT ASSESSMENTS

Over the years we have collected and/or deployed a wide variety of assessment surveys. Many we are in the process of converting to GroupMind Impression Capture™ templates, so that all that needs to be added to complete the customization are welcome language, introduction videos and of course related graphics. These include:

Strategic Speedometer (Strategic Speed™) – assesses degree to which the organization or business unit is paying attention to the people factors of clarity, unity and agility.

Leadership Practices (**Strategic Speed™**) – assesses degree to which the individual or team leaders are applying the four key leadership practices that are leading predictors of speed and success including a) **Affirming Strategies** b) **Driving Initiatives c) Managing Climate and d) Cultivating Experience**

Core Culture Assessment (IPS Learning-Stanford – now Twenty-Eight) – helps organizations identify their core culture, typically one of Control, Collaboration, Competence and Cultivation.

REFERENCES & AUTHOR BIOGRAPHIES

REFERENCES

1. Sull, Donald, Homkes, Rebecca, Sull, Charles, Why Strategy Execution Unravels – and What to Do About It. Harvard Business Review March 2015
2. Google OKR's Video Transcript 2013 and Doerr 1999
3. Koort, Külli, Turning Objectives into Results, weekdone.com 2016
4. Schwaber, Ken and Sutherland, Jeff, The Scrum Guide, The Definitive Guide to Scrum, Rules of the Game 2016
5. The Standish Group Report Chaos Report, 2014
6. Bossidy, Larry and Charan, Ram, Execution: The Discipline of Getting Things Done, Random House Business Books, 2011
7. Davis Jocelyn R., Frechette, Jr. Henry R., Boswell, Edwin H., Strategic Speed, The Forum Corporation, Harvard Business Press, 2010
8. Parker, John E., Using Lean, Agile and ITSM to Deliver Spectacular Results, EnFOCUS Solutions, Agile Webinar 2014
9. Majority of U.S. Employees Not Engaged Despite Gains http://www.gallup.com/poll/181289/majority-employees-not-engaged-despite-gains-2014.aspx, 2014
10. Clemson, Gaye I. & Leeds, Alan J., "A New Way to Drive Strategic Alignment in an Age of Disruption and Convergence", 2010 and "Lessons Learned in Driving Strategic Execution Through Effective Governance", 2015. ASP National Conference presentations.
11. Leeds, Alan J. Presentations
    a. American Society of Quality (ASQ), Silicon Valley Chapter: Agile strategy execution: The new Frontier
    b. Agile2016 Conference, Connecting the Dots: Linking Agile Strategy to Execution
    c. PMI Professional Development Day, Sonoma State University Connecting the Dots: Agile Strategy Execution, 2016
12. Leeds & Clemson, Linking Strategy to Execution through Innovative Techniques, The Strategic Execution Conference, IPS Learning and the Stanford Center for Professional Development 2014
13. The Economist Intelligence Unit Limited Why Good Strategies Fail – Lessons for the C-Suite, 2013
14. Converting Strategy Into Action Training, Stanford-IPS Learning
15. Web sites, GroupMind Express, AgileStrategyManager®, Q2E
16. Lechtenberg, Shannon and Ridderbusch, Greg, "From Stone Tablet to Web-Hosted Planning and Execution", Association for Strategic Planning National Conference, 2015
17. Bandrowski, Jim, Rock Your Industry to be published in 2017.
18. GroupMind White Papers Collection, www.groupmindexpress.com

AUTHOR BIOGRAPHIES

GAYE I. CLEMSON

Gaye I. Clemson is an award winning storyteller, communications and training innovator, culture change leader, organization performance metrics designer and strategic planning process facilitator, who brings many years of enterprise strategy and key initiative portfolio management expertise. She has held a number of functional roles in marketing, sales, international business and customer support. She currently leads Globalinkage Consulting, a consultancy that helps firms strengthen employee engagement, improve organizational performance and evolve operating models to enable innovative governance and decision-making processes. She speaks frequently at national and local industry conferences including most recently the NCHRA Global HR Summit, ASP National Conferences (2006, 2009 & 2015) the Bay Area's Strategy Execution Conference (Oct 2014). She is a published author of nine oral history narratives. She holds an Honours BCom from Queen's University at Kingston and is a Stanford Certified Project Manager.

ALAN LEEDS

Alan Leeds is the president of Agile Strategy Agile Strategy Manager, a strategy to execution software division of Y-Change Inc., a software company enabling progressive companies to convert strategy into reality. His expertise in agile strategy deployment, execution, change management methodologies and online software has helped companies deliver tangible operating results in organizations such as Raytheon, Cisco Systems, and Texas Instruments, Abbott Medical Optics and Great River Energy.

An ASP (Association for Strategic Planning) Certified Strategic Management Professional (SMP), Alan is also on their Board of Directors, and was inducted into their Hall of Fame in 2012. He was instrumental in the founding of the NorCal Chapter of the ASP. As a thought leader in strategic planning and agile strategy execution in the strategy community, he has produced high quality software tools for planners across the country. Alan holds a Masters degree from SUNY and a BS from Syracuse University. Alan's speaking engagements have included a presentation for the PMI conference at Sonoma State, several national conferences for the ASP, the most recent being at the Agile2016 conference in Atlanta. As an award-winning magician, he often incorporates magic into his presentations.

Made in the USA
San Bernardino, CA
19 January 2017